W9-BDX-686

Letters *from the* Battlefront

World War I

VIRGINIA SCHOMP

BENCHMARK BOOKS

MARSHALL CAVENDISH
NEW YORK

To Burt W. Phillips, U.S. Navy Reserves (Ret.),

and all our "peacetime warriors"

Benchmark Books
Marshall Cavendish
99 White Plains Road
Tarrytown, New York 10591-9001
www.marshallcavendish.com

Library of Congress Cataloging-in-Publication Data

Schomp, Virginia.
World War I / Virginia Schomp.
p. cm. — (Letters from the battlefront)
Summary: Describes the first World War through the letters of the people
who fought it, including doughboys, sailors, flying aces, and nurses.
Includes bibliographical references and index.
ISBN 0-7614-1661-7
1. World War, 1914-1918—United States—Juvenile literature. [1. World
War, 1914-1918—United States—Personal narratives.] I. Title: World
War 1. II. Title: World War One. III. Title II. Series: Schomp,
Virginia. Letters from the battlefront.

D570.S36 2004
940.4'8173—dc21   2003010444

Book design by Patrice Sheridan
Art Research: Rose Corbett Gordon, Mystic, CT
Cover: Gillian Jason Modern & Contemporary Art/Bridgeman Art Library
Bettmann/Corbis: pages 9, 13, 14, 19, 21, 27, 29, 39, 44, 50 & 72; SEF/Art Resource, NY: pages 10 & 35; Hulton Archive/Getty Image: pages 24, 30, 57, 67, 68, 75 & 79; Courtesy of the National Museum of the US Army: page 49; SuperStock: pages 53 & 70; Underwood & Underwood/Corbis: page 55; Erich Lessing/Art Resource, NY: page 59; AP/Wide World Photos: page 61; Lake County Museum/Corbis: page 80.

Printed in China
1 3 5 6 4 2

Contents

From the Author

Letters from the Battlefront is a companion to the *Letters from the Homefront* series. The books in that series told the story of America's wars from the viewpoint of those who worked, watched, and waited at home. These books look at the same conflicts through the eyes of the men and women on the front lines.

Historians often study letters and journals written by famous people—explorers, philosophers, kings—to gain information about the past. Recently they have discovered the value of writings by "ordinary" people, too. Students of history have begun to seek out and study the personal writings of farmers and merchants, slaves and slaveholders, sailors and foot soldiers. Documents such as these, often called primary sources, help us to understand the beliefs, hopes, and dreams of earlier generations and to learn how historical events shaped their lives.

This book uses primary sources to recapture the drama of life during World War I. In these pages you will meet the doughboys who fought on the western front, the sailors who patrolled the seas for German U-boats, and the flying aces who pioneered air combat. You will read the stories of African-American soldiers who struggled against racism and women who nursed the wounded in combat zones. Their letters and firsthand accounts create a portrait of patriotism, idealism, and courage. They introduce us to a generation that went to war convinced that its sacrifices would bring about a bright new world of freedom and lasting peace.

Introduction

The Great War

On June 28, 1914, Archduke Franz Ferdinand, heir to the throne of the Austro-Hungarian Empire, and his wife, Sophie, were assassinated in the Austrian province of Bosnia. Their killer was Gavrilo Princip, a nineteen-year-old Bosnian with close ties to a Serbian terrorist organization. A month later, Austria-Hungary declared war on Serbia. Soon millions of men in the uniforms of many nations were on the march. Two quick shots had set in motion one of the bloodiest wars in history.

The assassinations in Bosnia lit the fuse, but the underlying tensions that exploded into war had been smoldering in Europe for decades. The Continent's leading nations were intensely competitive. Since the late nineteenth century, they had often collided in their race to carve out empires both in Europe and abroad. Bitter rivalries had developed, along with a tangled web of secret military agreements and alliances. By 1914, Europe was divided into two armed camps. On one side were the Central Powers: Germany and Austria-Hungary. On the other were the nations of the Triple Entente, later known as the Allies: Great Britain, France, and Russia.

Russia and Austria-Hungary were particularly bitter enemies. For many years the two powers had squabbled over control of the Balkans, the region in south-eastern Europe that includes Serbia. When Austria-Hungary declared war on Serbia, Russia called out its troops. To support its ally, Germany declared war on

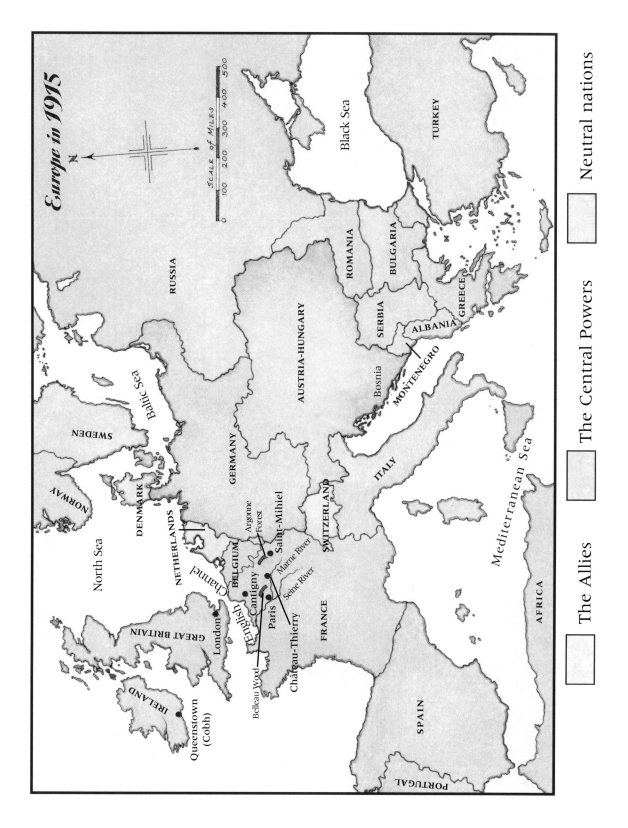

Europe in 1915

N

SCALE OF MILES
0   100   200   300   400   500

RUSSIA

Black Sea

TURKEY

ROMANIA

BULGARIA

GREECE

SERBIA

ALBANIA

MONTENEGRO

Bosnia

AUSTRIA-HUNGARY

GERMANY

Baltic Sea

SWEDEN

NORWAY

DENMARK

NETHERLANDS

North Sea

BELGIUM

English Channel

Argonne Forest

Saint-Mihiel

Marne River

Cantigny

Paris

Seine River

Château-Thierry

Belleau Wood

FRANCE

SWITZERLAND

ITALY

Mediterranean Sea

AFRICA

SPAIN

PORTUGAL

GREAT BRITAIN

London

IRELAND

Queenstown (Cobh)

The Allies   The Central Powers   Neutral nations

Russia. In turn, France and Britain honored their commitments by declaring war on the Central Powers. The "Great War"—known today as World War I—had begun.

The war's first blood was spilled in early August 1914, when Germany invaded neutral Belgium, on the road to France. Over the following weeks and months, Canada, Japan, Australia, and Italy would join the Allies, while Turkey and Bulgaria sided with the Central Powers. Altogether, fifty-seven nations on six continents would take part in World War I.

To Americans, the war in Europe seemed both horrifying and distant. A majority of Americans sympathized with the Allies. U.S. ties to Great Britain, with its common language and cultural traditions, and to the democratic government of France were especially strong. Nevertheless, the people of the United States were more than content to let Europeans fight their own battles. Shortly after the war broke out, U.S. President Woodrow Wilson declared that the nation would remain neutral, and most Americans applauded this isolationist policy.

As the war progressed, however, it would become increasingly difficult for Americans to remain on the sidelines. In time, the events in Europe would push the United States out of isolation, to the brink of war.

One

The Reluctant Warrior

*In the history of wars there is no single deed comparable in its
inhumanity and its horror to the destruction, without warning,
by German torpedoes of the great steamship Lusitania. . . .
Germany in her madness would have it understood that she is
at war with the whole civilized world.*

—THE NEW YORK TIMES, MAY 8, 1915

America Avoids Entanglements

"[We] need only keep our heads," the *New York Times* assured its readers in August 1914, "and go about our daily tasks with the determination to let war interfere with us as little as possible." Most Americans agreed. Since its founding more than a century earlier, the United States had always tried to steer clear of foreign entanglements. The war in Europe was a tragedy, declared the *Times*, but, like all distant conflicts, it was "a struggle we do not share."

8

The German army marches into Brussels, Belgium, in August 1914.

The first dent in America's armor of isolation came in late 1914, following Germany's invasion of Belgium. The British controlled the undersea cables that carried news from Europe to the States. Eager to build U.S. support for the Allied cause, they bombarded Americans with accounts of German atrocities against Belgian civilians. Some of the stories were true. Others were myths. Real-life tales of homelessness and starvation following the looting and burning of Belgian cities mingled with made-up horror stories of nuns assaulted and babies skewered on bayonets. Taken all together, the British propaganda created an image of German soldiers as "barbaric Huns" out to gobble up the world.

Responding to this propaganda, many Americans began to regard the Allies as the defenders of Western civilization. A victory by the Central Powers, they feared, could mean an end to democracy and freedom throughout Europe. While the

United States remained formally neutral, Americans donated hundreds of thousands of tons of food and other supplies to help "plucky little Belgium" resist its German invaders. U.S. businesses also loaned billions of dollars to the Allied nations.

At the same time, the struggles and suffering of Europeans still seemed safely distant from American shores. It would take a death-dealing German submarine to bring the realities of war closer to home.

The Sinking of the Lusitania

On May 1, 1915, the British luxury liner *Lusitania* steamed out of New York harbor for England. On board were 1,257 passengers, including 159 Americans. They enjoyed a pleasant ocean crossing, with calm seas and sunny weather. On May 7 hundreds gathered on deck for a first look at the green coast of Ireland. Suddenly a torpedo launched by a German submarine slammed through the ship's hull. The *Lusitania* sank in just eighteen minutes, carrying 1,198 people to their deaths.

Passengers escape the Lusitania, *sunk by German torpedoes on May 7, 1915. Germany's surprise attacks on unarmed civilian ships violated international law and moved the United States closer to war.*

CANADIAN JOURNALIST ERNEST COWPER WAS A PASSENGER ON THE FINAL VOYAGE OF THE *LUSITANIA*. WHEN THE TORPEDO STRUCK, COWPER SURVIVED BY LEAPING INTO THE WATER AND SWIMMING TO A LIFEBOAT. NEARLY A YEAR AFTER THE DISASTER, HE WROTE TO ELBERT HUBBARD II, WHOSE PARENTS WERE AMONG THE 128 AMERICANS KILLED ON THE *LUSITANIA*.

March 12, 1916

Dear Mr. Hubbard:

I should have written what I have written to you a long while ago—but I don't know, it seems as if the Lusitania left its seal on every one who was in it, and even now, almost a year later, I am afraid all the survivors are thinking more seriously of May 7, than they are of their business or the other things they should attend to. I know that is the case with me.

If you have been informed that there was a man on board who was in the company of your father and Mrs. Hubbard on many occasions, I guess they have me in mind, for we really did spend a lot of time together. . . .

Just a little before the torpedo hit us . . . I . . . called the attention of himself and Mrs. Hubbard to the extra watch which had been put on for submarines, and walked them forward to where two men were right at the stern with glasses. Two were on each side of the navigating-bridge, and three were in the crow's-nest, which is half way up the fore-mast. He expressed surprise at this, for he was sure a submarine would never make any effort to torpedo a ship filled with women, children and non-combatants. . . .

We then parted to go to our cabins before taking lunch. On finishing mine I went to the top deck, and was smoking . . . when I saw the torpedo coming toward us. . . .

I can not say specifically where your father and Mrs. Hubbard were when the torpedoes hit, but I can tell you just what happened after that. They emerged from their room, which was on the port side of the vessel, and came on to the boat-deck.

Neither appeared perturbed in the least. Your father and Mrs. Hubbard linked arms—the fashion in which they always walked the deck—and stood apparently wondering what to do. I passed him with a baby which I was taking to a lifeboat when he said, "Well, . . . they have got us. They are a damn sight worse than I ever thought they were."

They did not move very far away from where they originally stood. As I moved to the other side of the ship, in preparation for a jump when the right moment came, I called to him, "What are you going to do?" and he just shook his head, while Mrs. Hubbard smiled and said, "There does not seem to be anything to do."

The expression seemed to produce action on the part of your father, for then he did one of the most dramatic things I ever saw done. He simply turned with Mrs. Hubbard and entered a room on the top deck, the door of which was open, and closed it behind him. It was apparent that his idea was that they should die together, and not risk being parted on going into the water.

The blow to yourself and your sister must have been terrible, and yet, had you seen what I have seen, you would be greatly consoled, for never in history, I am sure, did two people look the Reaper so squarely in the eye at his approach as did your father and Mrs. Hubbard. . . .

Yours very faithfully,
Ernest C. Cowper

Primitive submarines had been used in combat as early as the American Revolution, but Germany was the first to develop and employ the sub as an effective tool of war. German submarines were called U-boats, short for *Unterseeboot*, or "undersea boat." The U-boats were Germany's answer to Great Britain's naval fleet, the largest in the world.

Early in the war the British navy had begun a blockade of German ports. British warships stopped and searched all foreign vessels entering the North Sea, confiscating weapons, gasoline, food, and other supplies that might aid the enemy. Germany went a step further with its submarine blockade. It proclaimed the waters around the British Isles a war zone. All vessels, including neutral merchant ships suspected of carrying war materials, would be sunk on sight.

On March 28, 1915, the first American died in World War I, as a passenger on a British ship torpedoed by a U-boat. On May 1 a German sub sank the U.S. oil tanker *Gulflight*. Six days later came the sinking of the *Lusitania*.

Americans were outraged by these attacks on innocent civilians. Under international agreements it was legal to destroy nonmilitary ships only if the passengers and crew were warned first and removed to safety. Germany's surprise attacks, President Woodrow Wilson argued, were a "violation of many sacred principles of justice and humanity." By September, Wilson's stern protests had forced Germany to call off its unrestricted U-boat campaign. Americans breathed a sigh of relief. The president had found an honorable solution to the crisis, and U.S. neutrality remained safe.

American Volunteers Abroad

After the sinking of the *Lusitania*, some Americans grew impatient with President Wilson's steady commitment to peace. Eager to punish Germany, tens of thousands of fiery young men enlisted in the British army or navy, French air force, or French Foreign Legion.

Other men and women joined volunteer organizations working abroad, such as the American Red Cross and the American Field Service. These volunteers served on the front lines in France, Serbia, and other war zones, driving ambulances and caring for the wounded. Among them was a young writer from Illinois, Ernest Hemingway. Hemingway served in the ambulance corps in France and Italy until July 1918, when he was wounded in an artillery attack. He later turned his experiences into one of the best novels ever written about World War I, *A Farewell to Arms*.

American Red Cross workers head for the battlefront in Europe.

All Eyes on Europe

While the United States avoided war, Europeans were fighting and dying by the hundreds of thousands. During the first months of the conflict, German troops sweeping through Belgium had met a determined French and British counteroffensive. By the winter of 1914, after several bloody battles, the exhausted enemy armies had stalled. All along the battlefront in western Europe, troops dug a double line of defensive trenches. The western front would eventually stretch nearly five hundred miles, from the English Channel all the way to Switzerland.

Meanwhile, in eastern Europe, German forces scored one victory after another over the Russian army. Bitter fighting in 1915 cost the Russians more than two million soldiers. The Allies also suffered more than 250,000 casualties in a disastrous assault on Turkey's Gallipoli Peninsula.

U.S. President Woodrow Wilson campaigned for reelection in 1916 promising to keep the country out of war.

Americans watched all these events with growing concern. President Wilson repeatedly tried to arrange peace talks, but the warring parties refused to even consider a compromise. As Wilson pursued peace, he also began to prepare for war. In late 1915 the president asked Congress to increase funding for the army and navy. The lawmakers responded by voting to expand American armed forces and build five new battle cruisers and other warships.

By late 1916, as the casualties continued to climb in Europe, Wilson's dreams of serving as a peacemaker were fading. Still, the president continued his commitment to neutrality. In November Americans showed support for his isolationist policy by electing him to a second term. Wilson had campaigned under the slogan "He Kept Us Out of War." Even the president, however, had doubts that he would be able to keep the promise implied by that slogan. "I can't keep the country out of war," he confided privately. "Any little German lieutenant can put us into war at any time by some calculated outrage."

America Declares War

On February 1, 1917, the German navy resumed unlimited submarine warfare. President Wilson reacted quickly, breaking off diplomatic relations with Germany. A few weeks later, the president handed journalists a document that would become known as the Zimmermann telegram.

THE ZIMMERMANN TELEGRAM WAS A CODED MESSAGE SENT BY GERMAN FOREIGN MINISTER ARTHUR ZIMMERMANN TO GERMANY'S AMBASSADOR IN MEXICO, WHICH WAS INTERCEPTED AND DECODED BY BRITISH INTELLIGENCE AGENTS. THE TELEGRAM INSTRUCTED THE DIPLOMAT TO MEET WITH MEXICO'S PRESIDENT AND PROPOSE AN ALLIANCE. IN RETURN FOR MILITARY SUPPORT AGAINST THE UNITED STATES, GERMANY WOULD HELP MEXICO REGAIN TERRITORY IT HAD LOST IN THE U.S.–MEXICAN WAR OF 1846–1848. THE MESSAGE ALSO SUGGESTED THAT MEXICO TRY TO PERSUADE JAPAN, WHICH HAD JOINED THE ALLIES, TO SWITCH SIDES. ON MARCH 1 THE ZIMMERMANN TELEGRAM MADE HEADLINES ACROSS THE UNITED STATES. AMERICANS WERE OUTRAGED, AND EVEN HOLDOUTS FOR NEUTRALITY BEGAN TO CLAMOR FOR WAR.

Jan 19 1917

We intend to begin on the first of February unrestricted submarine warfare. We shall endeavor in spite of this to keep the United States of America neutral. In the event of this not succeeding, we make Mexico a proposal of alliance on the following basis: make war together, make peace together, generous financial support and an understanding on our part that Mexico is to reconquer the lost territory in Texas, New Mexico, and Arizona. The settlement in detail is left to you. You will inform the President [of Mexico] of the above most secretly as soon as the outbreak of war with the United States of America is certain and add the suggestion that he should, on his own initiative, invite Japan to immediate adherence and at the same time mediate between Japan and ourselves. Please call the President's attention to the fact that the ruthless employment of our submarines now offers the prospect of compelling England in a few months to make peace.

Signed,
ZIMMERMANN

Coded Telegram

Decoded Message

In March German U-boats sank four U.S. merchant ships. Americans took to the streets, carrying banners reading LET'S GET THE HUN! ON TO BERLIN! "There is no question about going to war," thundered former president Theodore Roosevelt. "Germany is already at war with us."

Finally, on April 2, Woodrow Wilson addressed Congress. In a soft and solemn voice, the president who had spent nearly three years striving to preserve American neutrality asked for a declaration of war against Germany. "The world must be made safe for democracy," Wilson declared.

> It is a fearful thing to lead this great peaceful people into war, into the most terrible and disastrous of all wars, civilization itself seeming to be in the balance. But the right is more precious than peace, and we shall fight for the things which we have always carried nearest our hearts—for democracy, for the right of those who submit to authority to have a voice in their own governments, for the rights and liberties of small nations. . . . To such a task we can dedicate our lives and our fortunes, everything that we are and everything that we have, with the pride of those who know that the day has come when America is privileged to spend her blood and her might for the principles that gave her birth and happiness.

Nearly every sentence of the president's speech was punctuated with applause. Four days later, Congress formally approved a declaration of war.

Two

Yanks at War

Over there, over there,
Spread the word, send the word, over there,
That the Yanks are coming, the Yanks are coming, . . .
And we won't come back till it's over over there.

—"OVER THERE," SONG BY GEORGE M. COHAN, 1917

Americans Join the Fight

"On the 14th of April I made my decision to enter the Marine Corps," recalled Merwin Silverthorn of Minnesota.

The recruiting office was on the fourth floor of an office building. . . . That line, to get your name in the book, extended up the office down the hall and down four flights of steps, down on the sidewalk and around the corner—just to give you an idea of the enthusiasm.

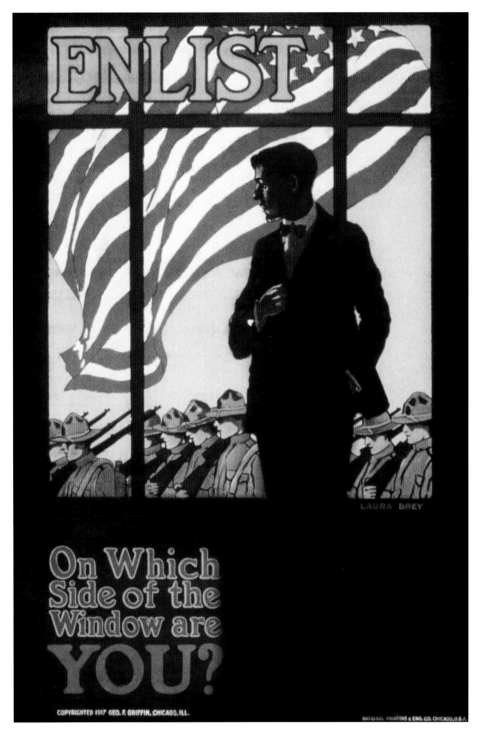

A recruiting poster urges American men to take part in the fight for democracy.

Thousands of enthusiastic young men joined America's armed forces in the first days after the declaration of war. Like college student Henry Villard, they were "fired by patriotic fervor, bent on helping to make the world safe for democracy." For many, there was another strong motive: the promise of adventure and heroism. "We could picture ourselves . . . pushing the Hun back from trench to trench," remembered Justin Klingenberger of West Virginia, "stopping only now and then to cut notches in the stocks of our rifles."

Despite America's war enthusiasm, it quickly became clear that an all-volunteer army could not meet the nation's needs. In May 1917 Congress passed the Selective Service Act, instituting the first conscription, or draft, since the Civil War. The law required all men aged twenty-one to thirty to register for active service.

Many people objected to conscription. They believed that involuntary military service was undemocratic and un-American. President Wilson responded that the war was an American undertaking, and therefore the draft was "in no sense a conscription of the unwilling: it is, rather, a selection from a nation which has volunteered in mass."

Schools for War

The first draft selection began in July 1917. By the year's end, U.S. armed forces numbered 750,000, including about 520,000 draftees and 230,000 volunteers. But new recruits expecting instant adventure were in for a disappointment.

"All of us . . . had visions of being rushed to the firing line," recalled infantryman Sam Woodfill. "We figured they'd shoot us across on the next boat. . . . Instead of sending us to war they sent us to school, to learn how to be soldiers, I guess."

To house America's "instant army," the government threw together thirty-two training camps. Early recruits arrived to find half-built wooden barracks and acres of canvas tents. Equipment was in short supply, too. Many men trained with wooden sticks for rifles and rocks for hand grenades. They practiced cavalry movements, recalled recruit Francis Field, on "long, hollow, wooden cylinders mounted on four sticks."

Despite these less-than-ideal conditions, the rookie soldiers trained hard and learned quickly. Rex Thurston described a typical day at an army camp in Texas.

We get up in the morning at 5:45 and must be dressed by 5:50. . . . Breakfast at six. . . . At 6:45 we are called out for drill, which continues until 11:45. . . . Dinner at twelve-fifteen. . . . After dinner we attend lectures on army rules, articles of war, war material and everything pertaining to the army. . . . At 5:30 we are called out for retreat. This is when the flag is lowered. The roll is called, arms inspected and every man is supposed to be slicked up, shoes shined, clothes clean.

After several months of this routine, U.S. troops felt more than ready for the front lines. They had learned how to construct trenches, handle rifles and bayonets, throw grenades, and braid barbed wire. Long hikes and drill exercises had made them fit and strong.

Enthusiastic American troops, finally done with basic training, embark on their voyage to Europe's battlefields.

Finally, the day came when the company bugler blew "To Arms." The men boarded trains for New York City or Newport News, Virginia, where troopships waited to carry them overseas. "We're ready to go in for the big thing—the real thing," one new soldier wrote with confidence. But, like infantryman Louis Ranlett, many were also "spellbound by the wonder of the fact that here I was actually going to war. . . . What was before me now?"

BETWEEN MID–1917 AND THE END OF 1918, ABOUT TWO MILLION AMERICAN SOLDIERS CROSSED THE ATLANTIC TO HELP MAKE THE WORLD "SAFE FOR DEMOCRACY." SOME WENT TO WAR RELUCTANTLY. MANY MORE, BOTH DRAFTEES AND VOLUNTEERS, WENT WITH PRIDE, CONFIDENCE, AND DREAMS OF GLORY. TWENTY-SIX-YEAR-OLD LESTER HENSLER OF OHIO EXPRESSED THIS "GUNG-HO" SPIRIT IN A LETTER TO HIS PARENTS IN 1917. TRUE TO HIS PROMISE, HENSLER WOULD "COME MARCHING HOME" SAFELY AT THE WAR'S END.

Dear Mother and Father

Well Mother, this is the proudest day of my life. We leave for "over there" tonight, and I am thankful that I can take a place among men who will bring freedom to the world. I do not want you to worry about me at all, for I am coming back and will be 100 percent better for having gone, for in the army one gains a knowledge of life, that is impossible to gain elsewhere.

All I want of you all is to "Keep the home fires burning" and it will not be long until we come marching home our mission accomplished. . . .

When you speak of me in France, do not do so with a heavy heart, do it in a proud way, for it is indeed, a thing any parent should be proud of.

I feel this way about it I would rather die in war, than to have stayed out and lived a "Coward" and a "Slacker" and Mother there are many of those and think just how their parents must feel when ask[ed] about their son or sons.

This is a man's game, and let me tell you Mother when Bat[tery] "E" 312 F.A. [Field Artillery] (which is recognized to be the best of Bat. Of Field Artillery in the U.S. army) starts in there is going to be a long line of Huns in line at roll call in hell for breakfast. . . . Well I will say good bye to all and "don't worry."

Love and best wishes
Your loving son Lester

A "Bridge of Ships"

U.S. troops made the crossing to Europe on a variety of transports: converted American cargo ships, British passenger liners or military vessels, German ships captured in U.S. ports at the war's start. The crossings lasted about two weeks. They were usually uneventful but uncomfortable. The soldiers' most common complaints were overcrowding, seasickness, and boredom. To pass the time, the men exercised, played cards, and staged boxing and wrestling matches. When their ships reached the waters patrolled by German U-boats, "abandon ship" drills were added to the routine. Guy Bowerman, who sailed in August 1917, observed during one drill that it would be "a long jump" from the ship's deck to the lifeboats below, "but I imagine that if we do have to jump, the water will come to meet us a good way if we only wait for it."

For protection from the U-boats, transports traveled in convoys. A typical convoy included several troopships plus two or more destroyers or battle cruisers and several small, swift torpedo boats or subchasers. If a submarine attacked, the battleships would quickly strike back with torpedoes and depth charges (bombs designed to explode when they sink to a certain depth).

Only two troop transports were sunk by torpedoes on their trip to Europe, and most of the passengers on those ships escaped to safety. The United States and its Allies had built a "bridge of ships," closing the gap between American forces and European battlefields.

"Lafayette, We Are Here!"

"We marched down the street," recalled U.S. Army Captain Carroll Swan. "Little children, tots two, three, and four years old, lined the sidewalks for blocks and patted our hands as we went swinging along, and cries of 'Good luck, soldier boys!' came from all sides."

U.S. troops arrived in France and Britain to a hearty welcome. Europeans cheered for the young soldiers they called "Yanks," "Sammies" (for Uncle Sam), or "Teddies" (for Theodore Roosevelt). The Americans preferred an old Civil War nickname; they called themselves "doughboys."

Paris held its first doughboy parade on the Fourth of July 1917. Enthusiastic crowds tossed wreaths and bouquets, wrote General John J. Pershing, until the troops "looked like a moving flower garden." The parade ended at the tomb of the Marquis de Lafayette, the young French nobleman who had fought with the Patriots in the American Revolution. There one of Pershing's officers spoke a few stirring words that thrilled the French and Americans alike: *"Lafayette, nous voici!—* Lafayette, we are here!"

General Pershing had been placed in command of the American troops in Europe, known as the American Expeditionary Force. The French and British wanted to send the Americans straight into action, as replacements scattered through the struggling Allied armies. Pershing had other plans. The stern-faced commander insisted that U.S. troops remain together. As convoys arrived, the men would be trained and organized into one vast independent army. Only that way could the Americans hope to mount "a successful offensive [that] would operate to defeat decisively the German Army."

Through the fall and winter of 1917, Pershing prepared his troops for frontline combat. The doughboys dug

U.S. General John J. Pershing (center) *inspects British troops in France.*

trenches in the sun and in the rain. They continued their training with bayonets, hand grenades, rifles, machine guns, and artillery. Then each battalion spent a few weeks with the French and British on the front lines, learning firsthand about trench warfare.

WEARY ALLIED TROOPS WERE CHEERED BY THE ARRIVAL OF THEIR NEW AMERICAN COM-RADES-IN-ARMS. MANY WERE ALSO STRUCK BY THE SOLDIERS' INNOCENCE AND CARELESS CONFIDENCE. WAR CORRESPONDENT FLOYD GIBBONS OBSERVED THE DOUGHBOYS' CASUAL ATTITUDE TOWARD WAR WHEN HE ACCOMPANIED THE COMMANDER OF A U.S. INFANTRY BAT-TALION ON AN INSPECTION TOUR OF THE FRONT LINES.

We walked up to a place where two Americans were standing on a firing step with their rifles extended across the parapet. They were silently peering into the grey mist over No Man's Land. One of them looked around as we approached. Apparently he recognized the Major's cane as a symbol of rank. He came to attention.

"Well," the Major said, "is this the way you let us walk up on you? Why don't you challenge me?"

"I saw you was an officer, sir," the man replied.

"Now, you are absolutely sure I am YOUR officer?" the Major said slowly and cold-ly, with emphasis on the word "your." "Suppose I tell you I am a German officer and these men behind me are Germans. How do you know?"

With a quick movement the American brought his rifle forward to the challenge, his right hand slapping the wooden butt with an audible whack.

"Advance one, and give the countersign," he said with a changed voice and manner and the Major, moving to within whispering distance, breathed the word over the man's extended bayonet. . . .

A hundred yards farther on, . . . a turn in the trench revealed to us the muffled fig-ures of two young Americans, comfortably seated on grenade boxes on the firing step.

From their easy positions they could look over the top and watch all approaches without rising. Each one had a blanket wrapped around his legs and feet. They looked the picture of ease. Without moving, one, with his rifle across his lap, challenged the Major, advanced him, and received the countersign. We followed the Major in time to hear his first remark:

"Didn't they get the rocking chairs out here yet?" . . .

"No, sir," replied the seated sentry. "They didn't get here. The men we relieved said that they never got anything out here."

"Nor the footstools?" the Major continued, this time with an unmistakable tone. . . .

"Do you two think you are taking moon baths on the Riviera?" the Major asked sternly. "You are less than two hundred yards from the Germans. You are all wrapped up like Egyptian mummies. Somebody could lean over the top and snake off your head with a trench knife before you could get your feet loose. Take those blankets off your feet and stand up." . . .

Stopping in front of a dugout, the Major gathered us about [and knocked] sharply on the door.

"Come in," was the polite and innocent invitation . . . spoken from below. The Major had his helmet on, so he couldn't tear his hair.

"Come up here, you idiots, every one of you." . . . There was a scurrying of feet and four men emerged carrying their guns. . . .

"At midnight," the Major began, "in your dugout in the front line forty yards from the Germans, with no sentry at the door, you hear a knock at the door and you shout, 'Come in.' I commend your politeness, and I know that's what your mothers taught you to say when visitors come, but this isn't any tea fight out here." . . .

All four decided to spend the remainder of the night on the firing step with their eyes glued on the enemy's line. They simply hadn't realized they were really in the war.

Doughboys at the Front

The "front line" was not a line at all. Instead, it was a long, complicated network of trenches that zigzagged across the countryside for hundreds of miles. There was a front-line trench guarded by machine guns and lethal tangles of barbed wire. Behind that were second-, third-, and sometimes even fourth-line trenches. Communication trenches led to the rear, providing routes for messengers and supplies. Stretching between the trench networks of the opposing armies was a strip of shell-torn earth known as no-man's-land.

The soldiers in the trenches lived in mud and filth. They slept in large holes dug out of the back of the trenches and reinforced with lumber. These dugouts varied

American infantrymen rest after capturing a portion of the German second-line trenches near Paris.

in size, holding anywhere from ten to fifty men. Cockroaches, lice, and foot-long rats were their constant companions.

Food was generally abundant in the trenches. The soldiers' diet included bread, butter, jam, rice, coffee, tea, and canned beef. They also ate "slum," described by one infantryman as a "haphazard melange of meat, vegetables, and whatnot." Water was scarce, with a canteenful a day serving for drinking and washing. "There was hardly any water for toilet [washing and grooming] purposes," remembered infantry officer Louis Ranlett. "Many of the men used coffee for shaving, both because it was hot and because it was more abundant than plain water."

Sept 10 1918

Dear Father & Mother—

*. . . Where I am now sitting, Jove if you could only peek in on me here. You would won-
der how humans could be so near like rats. Yet for us, it is quite comfortable much better than the average. we have a tiny stove, the pipe goes out the stair way. A little table,
and a grease lamp. . . . While it is very rainy and cold outside, we are getting along first
rate with a fire in our stove. I have a mattress on my cot. The rats tho dont seem to mind
where they go—just as leave run over your face at nite as try to get to your bread in the
daytime. I dont think they like me very well as I have my loaf of bread hung from the
ceiling on a wire and one thing a mouse or rat can't do, is climb down a wire to a loaf of
bread, which I am not at all sorry of. . . .*

*Well mom—I had a rather novel little experience last nite. While writing last
evening I stated that the bread was hung where a rat or mouse could not climb to it. Well
that is so—But—here is how it happened. Mr. rat comes bounding down stairs—and of
course by experience knew the bread was where he could not climb and get it, so
pounced on to my body, shoves in his toe nails and in one strenuous leap reaches his
goal—the loaf of bread. Of course when I felt him push I knew what was taking place.
. . . I was peeved at the nerve of the big brute—I slipped my hand over to the Colt .45
. . . , cocked it, and with my other hand used the flash light. Well the bright light made
him hesitate a second (they get so careless too, they take their time at whatever they do)
and that was a bit too long for him, for I let him have one lead pill. . . .*

*I do believe if any of you were placed in this bloody wet dugout, with all these pesky
rats, mice & lice, wet muddy trenches out side, no baths or change of clothes, shoes &
leggings all covered with this clay stuff, wet wood to burn, a measly little candle for
light, and thats not half of it, well I doubt if you would write as much as I do. Yet I am
"comfortable" for I am well, "happy"—for I get plenty of good eats and "contented"—
for I feel lucky to have even this much. . . .*

Paul

Life and Death in the Trenches

The doughboys' life was a mixture of boredom and terror. During the day men took turns peering through a periscope-like box over the top of the trenches toward the enemy lines. Sometimes they worked digging out and repairing sections of trench. After dark they might sneak out into no-man's-land to string barbed wire or to eavesdrop on enemy conversations. From time to time small parties raided the opposing trenches, hoping to capture prisoners and gather intelligence.

Day or night there was a constant threat of sniper fire. Raising a head above ground in daylight or showing a light at night could cost a careless doughboy his life. Enemy trench raids and periodic artillery attacks added to the danger. The most feared of all the threats, however, was poison gas.

The Germans first used this terrible new weapon in early 1915. Soon both sides had seized on poison gas as a tool for breaking down enemy defenses before an attack. Gas was usually released from shells fired by artillery. Some varieties were irritants that caused burning eyes, violent sneezing fits, or skin blisters. Other types of gas were lethal. Cyanide caused instant death. Phosgene damaged the lungs, killing its victims hours or even days after it was inhaled. One of the most dreaded of the "gases" was actually a yellow liquid known as mustard gas. It produced agonizing burns, lung damage, and temporary or permanent blindness.

A soldier and his horse. "Try putting a gas mask on one of them . . . under fire," said one artilleryman. "It was impossible!"

Both sides quickly developed gas masks to protect their troops. There were even masks for the horses and mules that pulled the artillery and supply wagons. These were less effective than the soldiers' masks. They were also a chore to put on. As artillery lieutenant Robert Casey explained,

> A horse without a gas mask can live about five minutes. With a gas mask he can live about five minutes. It takes only about eleven minutes to convince the horse that he ought to wear the gas mask. And there you are.

"Over the Top"

The trenches halted troop movements. The only way to advance was to go "over the top." Troops planning an advance usually softened up the enemy first with an artillery barrage. Artillery and mortar shells might be packed with explosives or with shrapnel that fell in a splintered metal rain over the opposing forces. There were also the deadly canisters loaded with poison gas.

A phosphorous bomb lights up the skies over no-man's-land. This type of bomb was filled with liquid phosphorous and oil, which ignited on impact.

ONE OF THE WORST PARTS OF TRENCH WARFARE WAS THE SENSE OF HELPLESSNESS SOLDIERS FELT DURING AN ENEMY ARTILLERY ATTACK. ROY BAINBRIDGE, SERVING WITH AN ARMY UNIT THAT TRANSPORTED AMMUNITION TO THE FRONT LINES, DESCRIBED HIS EXPERIENCES UNDER ENEMY FIRE.

July 18th 1918

Dear Mother—

Well there has been great activity in the line of warfare since my last letter. I never realized before that [so much] destruction of material things as well as human life could possibly occur in a few hours. . . .

One afternoon . . . , I and twelve or fifteen of the men in our company, were left in camp while the rest of the company were out delivering ammunition. Long range guns were dropping high explosive shells over us and scoring a few direct hits on the hospital. Now it is very seldom you hear the guns that fire these long range shells but on this occasion we could hear the guns that were firing these shells. The report [explosive noise] could be heard before the shell came over. . . . About three seconds after the report from the gun was heard then came the short shrill whine or whistle of the shell going over and then the explosion of the shell itself. These shells were falling only about three hundred yards over and beyond us and were going directly over us. We didn't feel much danger as the shells were going over and anyway there were few dugouts in this town so we were out lying on the grass. But later those gunners became careless with their range and shells started to drop first on one side and then another. . . .

Every time we heard the whistle of a coming shell we would duck just the same. This is a habit you very soon acquire. This whine of the coming shell can be heard two or three seconds before it hits. . . . It is certainly a helpless feeling that comes upon one when the shells come near and you are out in the open, on an open road, or halted on a shell swept road that is filled with traffic.

I am not writing this to show you the danger because all this does not happen every day. . . . The area of ground is so large that thousands of shells do nothing but dig holes in the ground. . . .

Your son
Corp. R. T. Bainbridge

After hours of artillery bombardment, the attacking troops climbed out of their trenches. They charged across no-man's-land straight into the defenders' machine-gun and rifle fire. The men who made it through that hail of death pounced down into the facing trenches, stabbing wildly with knives and bayonets. Sometimes they succeeded in capturing a portion of the trenches. More often they were beaten back by the enemy's defenses. Either way, assaults always ended in a terrible slaughter of men on both sides.

Rudolph Bowman was on the front lines in France, learning enemy observation techniques, when he "decided to go 'Over the Top' with the doughboys. . . . [It's] all confused to me—I saw many dead men. . . . [Men] fell around us, we were shot at by snipers, machine guns, . . . and went thru our own barrage twice." Later, Bowman remembered the experience as "awful—and wonderful—glorious—hideous—hellish."

Year of Crisis

The year 1917 was the most difficult yet for the Allies. More than two years of fighting had brought death and destruction to the war zones, hunger and suffering to the homefront. In March the discontented people of Russia staged a violent revolution. The Communist government that swept to power eventually negotiated a separate peace with Germany, ending Russia's involvement in the war.

The remaining Allies were also strained to the breaking point. In April 1917 French soldiers mutinied, refusing to make any more attacks on the German lines. In November the Italian army nearly disintegrated after disastrous losses in the Battle of Caporetto. That same month Britain ended a long offensive known as the Third Battle of Ypres (EE-per), after losing more than a quarter of a million men.

Through these dark days American troops continued to arrive and train for combat. But it would take months for General Pershing to build an army large and strong enough to play a significant role in the fighting. Meanwhile, 1917 would end with both sides still locked in an uneasy stalemate.

"I was talking to one of the fellows who was in the trenches this morning," wrote doughboy H. W. Ross.

In the quiet sector they were in, they say, the principal aim of both sides seemed to be to keep the peace. A French sentry told one of them: "If you see a German, don't shoot; you'll only start trouble." "Hell," said the American, "that's what we're here for."

Three

At Sea and in the Air

The duration of life at the front in the French aviation service is about sixty actual flying hours, and English statistics figure as low as forty hours. It is great sport, and all that I ask is that I be given a chance to take a few Boches [Germans] with me when I go.

—HENRY BREWSTER PALMER,
AMERICAN VOLUNTEER, FRENCH AVIATION SERVICE

Building an Antisubmarine Fleet

When the United States entered World War I, one of the greatest threats facing the Allies was the German submarine. Germany's blockade of Great Britain was highly effective. U-boats were sinking hundreds of thousands of tons of cargo headed for the British Isles each month. If the Allies could not stop the attacks, Britain would be starved out of the war and American troops would never reach Europe.

The U.S. Navy fleet numbered about three hundred ships, including more than fifty battleships and battle cruisers. Giant warships like these were the stars of every

Allied warships sink two Austro-Hungarian destroyers in one of the early sea battles of World War I.

major navy in the world. The U-boat menace forced a rethinking of America's naval strategy, however. Plans for building new battle cruisers were halted. Instead, U.S. shipyards began working on smaller, faster antisubmarine vessels such as destroyers, torpedo boats, and subchasers. A year after the declaration of war, America was turning out nearly four of these ships each day, and its fleet had grown to more than one thousand vessels.

The Queenstown Patrol

Unlike the independent American ground troops in Europe, U.S. naval forces worked closely with the Allied fleets. The first American ships in action were six destroyers rushed to Queenstown (present-day Cobh), Ireland, in late April 1917. Their orders were to "cooperate fully with the British Navy . . . in the protection of commerce near the coasts of Great Britain and France."

THE COMMANDER OF THE FIRST AMERICAN DESTROYERS IN EUROPE WAS JOSEPH KNEFLER TAUSSIG. COMMANDER TAUSSIG KEPT A DIARY OF HIS EXPERIENCES PATROLLING FOR GERMAN SUBMARINES OUT OF THE U.S. FLEET'S PORT IN QUEENSTOWN, IRELAND. IN THIS ENTRY FROM MAY 6, 1917, HE RECORDED TIPS ON ANTISUBMARINE WARFARE GIVEN BY BRITISH VICE ADMIRAL SIR LEWIS BAYLY TO THE AMERICAN CAPTAINS SHORTLY AFTER THEIR ARRIVAL IN EUROPE.

All Captains went to the Admiralty House where Admiral Bayly gave us a talk. . . . He said in substance that the problem before us was a serious one; that as soon as we pass beyond the defense of the harbor we face death until we return; there we must presume that a submarine is always watching us, and that although we may go for days without seeing a submarine or anything suspicious, we must not relax for an instant or we might lose our opportunity to destroy a submarine. . . . Stationary periscopes may be decoy mines; do not ram them but shell them; in picking up survivors of ships sunk beware of stopping until thoroughly convinced that no submarine is about; we must not risk the lives of our crews in order to save a few others; . . . if we see a ship struck, go after the submarine and let the rescue work wait. Our duty is: first, to destroy enemy submarines; second, to convoy and protect shipping; third, to save lives if we can. To miss an opportunity to sink a submarine means that he remains to sink other peaceful vessels and destroy more lives; . . . always zigzag or the submarine will plot your position; . . . on patrol do not patrol regularly from one end of the line to the other, but proceed irregularly so the submarine cannot establish the ship's position; . . . watch fishing vessels as they may be submarines in disguise; submarines frequently disguise themselves, using masts, and sails. . . . There were numerous other points which I do not now recall, but which I think made sufficient impression to be useful.

Days after their patrol began, the U.S. destroyers came across their first U-boat. The enemy sub was shelling two Allied sailing ships. The Americans opened fire, forcing the sub to flee, then picked up survivors from the Allied vessels. British newspapers applauded the U.S. Navy's introduction to the "submarine smashing game."

In time, the U.S. destroyer force guarding European waters would expand to eighty vessels. The Americans tangled with U-boats in some 250 actions, losing only one destroyer. Other U.S. ships escorted the troop transports and merchant vessels bringing soldiers and supplies to Europe. The navy also laid tens of thousands of mines in a huge arc across the North Sea, in an unsuccessful attempt to trap the U-boats in German ports.

A Sailor's Life

Daily life on a navy ship could be pleasant or uncomfortable, boring or exciting. It all depended on the weather, the type of ship, and the duty the crew was assigned.

On smaller ships such as destroyers and subchasers, rough seas often made the sailor's life miserable. William Duke, Jr., recalled a storm in December 1917 that rocked his ship for three endless days.

> The most tense moment of my life [was] when, while the seas were breaking over us and we were crawling about the deck holding fast to everything that seemed fixt, . . . we suddenly discovered that six [depth charges] had become unloosed and were lurching about. . . . These mines are controlled by the paying out of wire, and when a certain amount becomes uncoiled they automatically explode. As no man knew just how much wire had become unmeshed we all had to work fast heaving them overboard, and they went "pop, pop, pop," as quickly as champagne corks at the French Ball.

John Jordan, a crew member on a subchaser patrolling the Mediterranean Sea, described his ship as "small but mighty. . . . [The chasers] ride worse than a horse or mule and rock and roll like a cradle." Despite the discomforts Jordan enjoyed "many thrilling experiences" spotting submarines and engaging in battle. The day his unit of chasers located a U-boat base on the coast of Spain, he recalled, was one "I never shall forget. It sure was some experience to see those Germans beat it and we after them."

Conditions were generally less exciting—and more comfortable—on the giant battleships that joined the British Grand Fleet in its blockade of German ports. The German fleet, outnumbered nearly two to one, rarely challenged the Allied warships. Still, battleship crews were proud to play a role in maintaining the Allies' all-important mastery of the seas. "It was the policy of the Grand Fleet," recalled American commander Hugh Rodman,

> to go after the enemy every time he showed his nose. . . . Whether he appeared with single ships, divisions, or his whole fleet, out we went after him, by day or night, in rain or shine . . . , blow high, blow low—and chased him to his hole.

Knights of the Air

Air warfare was born in World War I. The airplane was a new invention, having made its appearance just a decade earlier. At first, both sides used their primitive wooden flying machines solely for observing enemy movements and spotting artillery targets. In 1915 pilots began mounting machine guns within reach of their open cockpits. Soon improved metal aircraft were staging attacks on enemy troops, factories, and supply dumps, using guns, grenades, and light bombs.

The fledgling U.S. Army Air Service had only about 1,200 men and fewer than three hundred planes, none suitable for combat. But thousands of Americans were eager to join the war in the air. In the first year of U.S. involvement, nearly 40,000 young men applied to join the air service. Only half met the service's strict standards, which included high intelligence, a "good eye for distance, keen ear for familiar sounds, steady hand and sound body" as well as "a cool head in emergencies." Those who were accepted trained mainly in British or French flight schools, flying French-made planes. Graduates would join an elite group of men often looked up to as "knights of the air."

Aces and Dogfights

"Here one could not ask for better conditions. All we do is eat, sleep and fly," wrote air service trainee Kramer Table in France. American "flying cadets" went through an intensive training program designed to turn out seasoned pilots in just three to four months. Most of the men had never been in a cockpit before. Yet within weeks, they were practicing the techniques that could help them survive in combat: spotting enemy aircraft, firing their plane's machine gun, performing "acrobatic" loops, spins, turns, spiral climbs, and nose dives.

Allied and German biplanes engage in aerial combat.

Americans Earn Their Wings

For U.S. Army Air Service cadets, flight training was highly exciting and extremely dangerous. Early combat planes were frail and unreliable. An engine might conk out or catch fire. Wings tore or sometimes fell off completely. Inexperienced pilots collided in foggy weather, got lost and ran out of fuel, or crashed while practicing turns and dives. Some fell to their deaths—there were no parachutes for plane pilots at the time.

Lieutenant Samuel Mandell had an unforgettable experience flying a two-seater during a group training exercise.

> *I heard a sort of crash behind. . . . Lo and behold, a man in a leather coat [was] holding onto the tail of my machine. I could hardly believe my eyes, but Fiske had fallen out of his cockpit when his gun broke loose from its fastenings. . . . As I watched him over my shoulder, he gradually wound his way up the fuselage. He got a-straddle of it and gradually slid up, . . . and dove head first into his seat.*

Nearly half of the Americans accepted into the air service cadet program were killed, seriously wounded, or declared unfit for flying before they finished their training. For those who earned their wings, the thrill of "conquering the air" outweighed all the risks. "The day of days has come!" wrote one young pilot after completing his training and joining a squadron "in the Field in France. . . . Now I'm right in the Great Adventure, of fighting the war in the air, and wondering where it will all lead."

IN THE AUTUMN OF 1917, EIGHTEEN-YEAR-OLD JACK MORRIS WRIGHT ARRIVED AT FLIGHT-TRAINING SCHOOL IN TOURS, FRANCE. A FEW DAYS LATER, THE YOUNG AMERICAN WROTE TO HIS MOTHER IN NEW YORK, SHARING THE THRILLS AND DANGERS OF LEARNING TO FLY. JACK WRIGHT DIED IN JANUARY 1918, WHEN HIS PLANE STALLED AND CRASHED DURING A PRACTICE LANDING.

September 11, 1917

My Very Dear Mother:

I don't know just what to say to you—I don't know just what to say to myself! I have arrived at camp and don't know what to make of it. . . .

We get up at 5 A.M. (awful), have breakfast and get out to the field by 6.30 when we start flying until 9.30. . . . Then we have a lecture until 10.30 and lunch at 11. From 11 to 3 P.M. we have absolute rest, and, believe me, we need it! I have found out that flying is going to be not only tiring but strenuous. . . .

You have to go through numerous schools. First you just follow the movements of your pilot; then he lets you gradually take control until he perfects you in the landing school. Landing is the most delicate of all flying. Then you go into the solo class; then the spiral, the triangle, and finally, graduate at the end of a time proportionate with the weather, and receive your First Lieutenant's commission. . . .

The first evening I walked from the dinner table out about twenty yards to where stretched the main field, and where, forbidden sight, men came swooping down or went soaring up almost within hand's reach. What I had found such a rare treat in the movies was now going on before my eyes in reality; but I could hardly believe that this was actually the heroic, dreadful, sublime aviation school and that these mere boys who came joking along with their big helmets in one hand were not more than the mere puppets of actual student-pilots. Was it possible that this boy whom I had studied Latin with . . . was the man of to-day, and the one on whom the Government was spending a little fortune [so] that within a few months he might be one of those most vital single factors in the war? That Bill was conquering the air, and that all of them could do so much was quite beyond me. But then I felt myself grow bigger; I knew that never had I faced such danger, and yet I was not afraid. Before I had been frightened by exams, [sports] matches, people, but now I felt myself rise above fear through the immensity of nobleness that such danger invoked. . . .

Now I have been here four days, and . . . have seen four accidents, of which one might have proved fatal, since he cut the wings off on some trees and spiked head first into the road. They don't let you get near the machine, though, for the sight of a friend hurt or killed would be bad for a beginner. . . .

Most lovingly, from your devoted aviator
Jack

When their training was complete, flyers went to the front to join the Allies in their struggle for mastery of the skies. The American airmen bombed German troops and ammunition dumps. They scouted out enemy troop movements and shot down enemy observation balloons. Most often, they engaged in air combat, or "dogfights," with German flight patrols.

The men in the trenches were thrilled by the sight of the daring Allied airmen dueling with enemy aviators overhead. "I have seen several air fights now, and three planes come down in flames," wrote artilleryman Bryan Turner in July 1918. "It's the biggest show I ever witnessed." Soldiers and civilians alike regarded the flyers as modern-day versions of the heroic knights of old. These "airborne warriors," wrote British fighter pilot Arthur Gould Lee, "engaged in single combat, like the knights . . . , but wielding a winged machine-gun in place of lance and sword."

Most honored of all pilots were the "aces"—those who shot down at least five enemy aircraft. Each of the warring nations had its top aces. U.S. pilot Eddie Rickenbacker was responsible for twenty-six "kills" following America's late entry into the war. Canada's Billy Bishop was credited with seventy-two, Britain's Edward Mannock with seventy-three, France's René Fonck with seventy-five. Leading them all was Germany's Baron Manfred von Richthofen. The "Red Baron" scored eighty victories before he was shot down and killed behind enemy lines in April 1918. In keeping with air combat's knightly code, the Allies gave their downed rival a full military burial, with British casket bearers and an Australian honor guard.

AMERICAN AND EUROPEAN NEWSPAPERS WERE FILLED WITH ACCOUNTS OF THE DARING EXPLOITS OF THE FLYING ACES. HUNDREDS OF OTHER PILOTS FLEW THEIR TINY, FRAGILE PLANES ON HAZARDOUS MISSIONS WITHOUT APPLAUSE OR FAME. ARTHUR GOULD LEE WAS ONE OF THESE "ORDINARY YOUNG MEN DOING THEIR JOB WITHOUT THOUGHT OF GLORY." WRITING TO HIS WIFE IN JUNE 1917, LEE DESCRIBED A NEARLY FATAL ENCOUNTER WITH A SQUADRON OF ALBATROSES. THE ALBATROS WAS A HIGHLY EFFECTIVE GERMAN FIGHTER, SOMETIMES CALLED THE "V-STRUTTER" FOR ITS V-SHAPED WING SUPPORTS.

Saturday, June 2nd

Did you ever hear of a frightened hawk? That was me this morning. One minute a cruel hawk pouncing on its prey, the next a fledgling, diving frantically to escape a flock of bigger and better hawks.

I was [flying] with Joske at nine o'clock. . . . We saw white archie [antiaircraft fire] to the south, potting at a Hun two-seater going south-east, well below. Joske started to go down, and I tailed along. . . .

I heard a loud and rapid crak-ak-ak-ak-ak-ak. I saw and smelt tracers whizzing by me, and there was a splash on the instrument board as my height indicator became a tangle of metal.

I looked around, startled to death, and there, thirty yards behind my tail, was a V-strutter with . . . his two guns flashing. They stopped, and in a split second I saw the pilot's head cocked to the side of the windscreen, checking to see if I'd been hit. Above him was a flock of other Albatroses.

Long before that split second was up I'd jerked the joystick forward and was on my way down with engine full on. . . . It was a thing I could never have done in cold blood, but with bullets cracking around my head I only thought of getting away. I was scared. I was diving at such a pace that my speed-indicator needle went off the dial, and stayed there. . . .

They were taking it in turns to dive and pot at me. Tracers flashed by in all directions, to the tune of repeated bursts of gunfire. Every burst made me cringe into the cockpit. I daren't look round again, I had to play being dead in a machine diving out of control. The wires screamed above the roar of the engine. The whole machine shuddered, as though about to break up. . . .

The ground rushed up at me, and I knew I must level out, bullets or no bullets. At that moment, thank heaven, the firing stopped. They'd decided I was a certain goner. I pulled the throttle back very gently, and kept in the dive until it was safe to ease out in a big curve. I leveled off at 500 feet, and I'd come down from 12,000. . . .

Surprisingly, there wasn't a lot of damage [to the plane]. . . . Though twelve guns had fired at me at their leisure, my rigger could only find twenty-nine bullet holes, seventeen in the fuselage, the rest in the wings. At first I concluded that the bullet which had smashed the height indicator must have travelled right through me without my noticing it, but when I took off my muffler I found it had gone through that and my flying-coat collar.

Airpower's Role

Despite its glamorous image, air combat was a deadly business. The odds of survival were even lower for pilots than for the doughboys in the trenches. In the final months of the war, the high casualty rates led to changes in the style of air warfare.

Flying ace Eddie Rickenbacker became an American hero, shooting down twenty-two enemy planes and four observation balloons.

One-on-one dogfights gave way to mass combat. Large formations flying together increased the pilots' chances of survival and proved more effective against the enemy. Hundreds of planes might fill the skies during an offensive, supporting an infantry attack, attacking enemy troops or guns on the battlefield, and bombing military or civilian targets.

These mass offensives, Arthur Gould Lee lamented, left "neither chance nor mood for knightly attitudes." However, they made the airplane an even more powerful weapon. Airpower would play an important role in the war's outcome and in all later wars. Today fighter pilots still use many of the basic techniques developed by the pioneering fighter pilots of World War I.

Four

African Americans and Women at War

If the colored citizens of the country seize this opportunity to emphasize their American citizenship by effective war activities, they will score tremendously. When men fight together and work together and save together, this foolishness of race prejudice disappears.

—AFRICAN-AMERICAN LEADER W. E. B. DUBOIS,
JULY 1918

African Americans Join the Military

Many patriotic African-American men were eager to serve their country in World War I. However, the idea of large numbers of blacks in the military worried political leaders.

Black men had served with honor in the nation's fighting forces since the days of the American Revolution. Still, racial prejudice and discrimination remained deeply rooted in American society. Many white Americans were convinced that black Americans lacked the intelligence, discipline, and courage needed to make good soldiers. They also feared that military service might make blacks less submissive, or even dangerous. Arguing against black conscription, Senator James Vardaman of Mississippi warned, "Millions of negroes who come under this measure will be armed. I know of no greater menace to the South than this."

Despite these misgivings, the Selective Service Act of May 1917 provided for drafting both whites and blacks. The nation desperately needed soldiers, and it could not afford to waste able-bodied men. Altogether, some 400,000 black soldiers would serve in World War I—the largest group yet of African Americans in the U.S. military.

FROM THE MOMENT THE GOVERNMENT DECIDED TO INCLUDE MEN OF ALL RACES IN THE DRAFT, AFRICAN-AMERICAN LEADERS BEGAN CAMPAIGNING FOR THE TRAINING OF BLACK OFFICERS. IN MAY 1917 A COMMITTEE OF BLACK RELIGIOUS AND CIVIC LEADERS SENT THIS LETTER TO PRESIDENT WILSON, ASKING FOR HIS SUPPORT. TWO MONTHS LATER, THE ARMY AGREED TO SET UP A SEGREGATED OFFICERS' TRAINING CAMP. DISCRIMINATORY RULES, HOWEVER, SHARPLY LIMITED THE NUMBER OF AFRICAN AMERICANS WHO COULD BECOME OFFICERS, RESTRICTED THEM TO THE LOWER RANKS, AND MADE CERTAIN THAT FEW WOULD EVER BE ASSIGNED TO ACTIVE DUTY

May 11, 1917

Honored Sir:
The undersigned, representing "The Committee of 100 Colored Citizens on the War", composed of representatives of numerous civic and religious organizations, . . . are petitioning the War Department to establish a special officers' training camp for the training of Colored officers for the Colored regiments in the New Federal Army. . . .

The War Department deemed it in-advisable to admit Colored men to the fourteen regular training camps and suggested a separate camp. Our young men are so anxious to serve their country in this crisis that they are willing to accept a separate camp. Fifteen hundred qualified men have already made application for admission to such a camp and their applications are in the hands of the Secretary of War. . . .

This opportunity for our representative young men to receive training as officers is not only necessary for the proper efficiency of the army but it is also essential to the

active and hearty patriotism of ten million Colored citizens. They stand ready to give themselves and all they possess, to this noble cause to which the nation has dedicated itself but they need the encouragement of a fair opportunity to demonstrate their loyalty on the field both as privates and as officers.

We feel assured that you will sympathize with us in our petition and we most respectfully request you to bring the matter favorably to the attention of Secretary of War [Newton] Baker before it is finally settled to-morrow. . . .

Most respectfully yours,
The Committee of 100 Citizens on the War

"Laborers in Uniform"

"Colored troops . . . are nothing more than laborers in uniform," maintained a top military officer in early 1918. "White men released by them from day labor work [can be] instructed for combatant service."

Unwilling to trust black troops in combat, the army assigned most to manual labor. Three out of four African Americans in uniform belonged to stevedore or labor companies. Stevedores loaded and unloaded the cargo of ships in port. Laborers loaded and unloaded trucks, built docks and warehouses, hauled coal and wood, dug ditches, carted garbage, and cared for the horses and mules. African Americans were segregated in all-black regiments, largely commanded by white officers.

Although the black troops were treated like second-class soldiers, the jobs they performed were vital to the war effort. The American Expeditionary Force needed an enormous quantity of food, clothing, ammunition, and other supplies to keep fighting. African Americans were among the first troops rushed to France in the summer of 1917 to start those supplies flowing. Their work was backbreaking and endless. To unload a giant cargo ship, stevedores might work day and night, in sixteen-hour shifts. One journalist was amazed to witness a work crew unload "five thousand tons in one day, when those Continental [European] wiseacres had calculated that . . . we might move 6000 tons in a month! . . . The victory that we are going to win will not be an all-white victory by any manner of means."

Black Troops at the Front

African-American soldiers were eager to prove themselves on the front lines. Most never got the chance. Some 200,000 black doughboys were sent to France, but only about 40,000 were assigned to combat. Black combat soldiers belonged to two infantry divisions: the Ninety-second and Ninety-third.

The Ninety-second Infantry Division was made up of draftees. The troops were poorly trained and equipped, and they were led by inexperienced officers. During the division's first battle, in September 1918, one of its regiments retreated. White

African-American doughboys proved their fighting spirit in fierce combat during the final months of the war.

commanders labeled the entire division "rank cowards." Many pointed to the incident as proof that black soldiers were not suited for combat.

The Ninety-third Infantry Division included both draftees and more experienced National Guardsmen. It was assigned to the army of France. The French welcomed the fresh troops gladly and treated them as equals. Serving under French leadership, all four regiments of the Ninety-third Division distinguished themselves in battle.

One of those regiments, the 369th, earned a nickname for its spirit and daring: the Hell Fighters. The men of the Hell Fighters regiment spent 191 days on the front lines, longer than any other American fighting unit. In September 1918 they took the lead in an American assault on German positions in France's Argonne

The Hell Fighters are honored for exceptional bravery in battle.

An Army of Immigrants

At the start of World War I, one-third of the U.S. population of about 100 million people were immigrants or the children of immigrants. That fact worried government leaders. Were these people patriotic Americans or were their loyalties divided? Especially suspect were the six million Americans of German ancestry, who endured prejudice, harassment, and violence at the hands of "superpatriots" throughout the war.

In nearly all cases the suspicions were groundless. German Americans and other groups of immigrants and Americans of foreign descent proved themselves steadfastly loyal. Millions served in the U.S. armed forces. Infantry Sergeant Alvin York recalled that his platoon was "mixed up from 'most every country. . . . A heap of them couldn't talk our own language at all."

To make certain the doughboys knew enough English to perform their military duties, army training camps set up language schools. There were also schools for the 31 percent of recruits who were illiterate. Most soldiers were eager to learn. Chaplain Evan Edwards recalled one soldier, however, who constantly cut his classes in "Early English."

> *I sought him out, and on his own confession that he couldn't write and could barely read, gave him a 15-minute talk on the value of an education. It was a fine talk. I waited for a reply. "Hell, Chaplain," he said, "I am going over there to shoot Germans, not to write letters to 'em!"*

Forest. Advancing from one shell hole to the next under heavy enemy fire, the Hell Fighters used their rifles and grenades to drive out the enemy.

France awarded the Hell Fighters the Croix de Guerre, its highest regimental decoration for courage in action. The Ninety-third Division's 372nd Regiment also won the Croix de Guerre, for its "superb spirit and an admirable scorn of danger." Along with these regimental awards, the men of the Ninety-third won more than five hundred French medals for individual acts of heroism. The costs of the black doughboys' courage were high: nearly one-third of the division's 10,000 men were killed or wounded in combat.

When their service ended, African Americans returned home to prejudice and discrimination. In the South a number of black veterans were beaten or driven out of town by racist whites who feared that the returning soldiers had been "infected" with ideas of liberty and equality. Some were murdered by white lynch mobs. The violence stamped out any hope of reward for the black troops' contributions to their country. But the wartime experiences of African Americans had increased their confidence, self-reliance, and determination to achieve their full rights and freedoms. "We return from fighting. We return fighting," proclaimed civil rights leader W. E. B. DuBois. "Make way for Democracy! We saved it in France, and by the Great Jehovah, we will save it in the United States of America, or know the reason why."

Women in the War Effort

World War I brought changes and challenges for American women. As men left for the front lines and the nation geared up to produce the tools of war, more than one million women took jobs in factories and shipyards. "Farmerettes" took the place of male farm laborers. Clerks and secretaries filled in for male government workers.

Tens of thousands of women joined the doughboys "over there." The majority of these volunteers served as nurses or supported the troops through organizations such as the American Red Cross or YMCA (Young Men's Christian Association). Others belonged to a revolutionary new class of American women: the first ever enlisted in the armed forces.

An American Red Cross volunteer and a Polish-American soldier in France. "Right up under the guns, you see these women with their baskets serving to the doughboys," wrote one soldier.

LIKE THE YOUNG AMERICAN MEN WHO FOUGHT FOR ALLIED ARMIES BEFORE 1917, SOME AMERICAN WOMEN WERE TOO IMPATIENT TO WAIT FOR THEIR COUNTRY TO JOIN THE WAR. THESE INCLUDED A YOUNG WOMAN KNOWN ONLY AS "MADEMOISELLE MISS." THE DAUGHTER OF A U.S. NAVAL OFFICER, SHE WAS IN FRANCE WHEN THE GREAT WAR BROKE OUT AND VOL-UNTEERED TO SERVE AS A NURSE WITH THE FRENCH RED CROSS. IN 1916 A COLLECTION OF LETTERS WRITTEN BY MADEMOISELLE MISS TO A FRIEND BACK IN THE STATES WAS PUBLISHED TO RAISE FUNDS FOR FRENCH MILITARY HOSPITALS.

October 8, 1915

You know how it is in the trenches, load and fire most of the time. That's how it is here. During the last week, we have averaged 25 operations daily. One day we had 33, and if you have any conception of an operating-room where they are short of assistants, you may know there was not much time left over. But the struggle, and the sense that one is saving bits from the wreckage, doesn't give one a chance to be mastered by the unutter-able woe.

In these days I have lost four, . . . and several others are in a desperate condition. I have never left my ward except for six hours' sleep each night, and one hour yesterday when I walked behind the [funeral] bier in the nurse's post of honor. . . .

I haven't the time nor the heart to tell you the tale of my days, but I tell you this, that I shall never get hardened to last agonies and heart-broken families. And when my lit-tle No. 23 flung out his arms last night to say "Good-by" (he knew he was going) "O, my sister, my sister! kiss me!" I tell you it took control to finish giving the last of my 34 anti-tetanus injections a few minutes later. . . .

Speaking of injections, please send me some platinum needles, big and little. I hope you will send cotton and gauze soon, and rubber gloves, too. . . . As for what is being done over there for these poor men, I can only say, God bless all the generous donors! None can imagine what the help will mean. Why, daughters of France could not have done more!

Supporting the Troops

"The cannon goes day and night and the shells are breaking over and around us," American nurse Florence Bullard wrote from a hospital in France. "As yet I have never had a moment's fear, but one is so busy and with hand and heart too full to think of your own self."

Some American nurses overseas were assigned to large, well-equipped base hospitals away from the combat zones. Others worked at casualty clearing stations near the front or field hospitals just out of range of enemy artillery. These women shared the hardships and dangers of war with the wounded men they tended.

British nurses treat a wounded soldier in the trenches.

Florence Bullard worked at a clearing station set up in "a sort of coal-cellar, completely underground" for protection from artillery attacks. The conditions were cramped and uncomfortable, with "no air, artificial light, and the cots . . . so close together you can just get between them." Helen Fairchild, a nurse from Pennsylvania, wrote from her station near Ypres, France, "We all live in tents and wade through mud to and from the operating room where we stand in mud higher than our ankles."

In these primitive surroundings nurses helped the doctors perform emergency surgery, bandaged wounds, dispensed food and medication, and prepared patients for transport to the rear. Sometimes all they could offer was comfort. About one-third of the men who reached the casualty clearing stations died from their wounds or from infection brought on by the filthy conditions.

Thousands of other women brought comfort to the troops overseas through the Red Cross, YMCA, Salvation Army, and other service organizations. Volunteers with these groups distributed hot coffee, donuts, chocolate, cigarettes, and newspapers to the men in the trenches. They set up clubs behind the lines where soldiers could relax, play games, dance, and listen to music. At YMCA dances there might be fifty men to each volunteer. The women switched partners every time a whistle blew. Despite the many army shoes trodding on dancing slippers, "somehow the girls endured it and kept smiling." To George Lee, a doughboy serving in France, the YMCA and Red Cross were "both wonderful organizations. The Y.M.C.A. is our only home and the Red Cross girls our mothers."

Women in the Military

More than 30,000 American women served in the U.S. Navy, Army, and Marine Corps during World War I.

The U.S. Navy swore in America's first enlisted women in March 1917. More than 11,000 women answered the navy's call to "Free a Man to Fight." Most of these "Yeomanettes" performed clerical work such as typing and bookkeeping. A few got a chance to prove their skills as electricians, chemists, photographers, fingerprint experts, torpedo assemblers, and camouflage designers. The majority of navy women served in the States, while a handful were sent overseas.

This recruiting poster for the U.S. Navy features a uniformed "Yeomanette."

Women in the U.S. Army served as nurses at frontline hospitals and base camps and on hospital trains and transport ships. The army also sent more than 200 French-speaking American women to France to work as "switchboard soldiers"—telephone operators at American Expeditionary Force headquarters.

The U.S. Marine Corps was slow to accept the idea of enlisting women. In the summer of 1918, severe manpower shortages finally forced the marines' top commander to ask for a report on what jobs, if any, women could handle. The answer surprised him. Senior Marine Corps officers estimated that women could perform 40 percent of the noncombat work done by men, although it would take three women to replace every two men.

Beginning in August 1918, 305 women were enlisted as privates in the Marine Corps Reserves. All were assigned to office work in the States. The marines made the most of its female personnel's publicity value, training them in military drills so they could march in parades and make other public appearances. One fact the Marine Corps did not publicize: it turned out that *two* women could do the work previously handled by *three* men.

Women were not offered the opportunity to remain in the armed forces after the war. The door had been opened, but it would be more than twenty years before women found a permanent place in the U.S. military. Nevertheless, their wartime service, both in the military and on the homefront, did result in one major advance. In June 1919 Congress acknowledged their contributions by passing the Nineteenth Amendment to the Constitution, granting women the vote.

Five

The Tide Turns toward Victory

Last night I witnessed a truly pitiful sight—the burying of our boys. The sight of our comrades being laid away for their final rest, garbed in a U.S. uniform, makes one's blood run cold and increases a passionate desire to deal out misery to the enemy—and I believe before this war is over he will have had more misery than he bargained for.

—AMERICAN SOLDIER LEO CUTHBERTSON,
JULY 25, 1918

Germany's Final Offensives

At the start of 1918, the mood was grim on both sides of the western front. The balance of war seemed to have tipped against the Allies. Russia had withdrawn from the fighting, and British, French, and Italian forces were exhausted. The Central Powers were also desperate. The Allied blockade was strangling Germany and its war partners. If they did not win a decisive victory soon, they would run out of the food and other supplies needed to carry on the fight.

Allied forces went on the defensive. They would conserve their troops and try to hold on until enough American soldiers arrived to tip the balance in their favor. Meanwhile, Germany's military commanders prepared for a full-scale attack. They knew that the American army was not expected to reach full strength until the summer. Before then, they intended to smash the Allies with a knockout blow on the western front.

The great offensive began on March 21, 1918. First came a shattering artillery bombardment along a forty-mile front south of the town of Arras, France. Then more than 750,000 specially trained storm troopers and other German infantrymen tore through the British and French defenses.

A German artist, toward the end of the war, painted this painful scene of his war-weary countrymen resting along a roadside.

The Allies were outnumbered nearly four to one in some areas. In less than a week, the Germans pushed them back forty miles. The devastating advance continued through the spring. By the end of May, German forces had reached the banks of the Marne River, just fifty miles from Paris.

Yanks to the Attack

When the Germans began their spring offensives, fewer than 300,000 U.S. troops had reached France. General Pershing still planned to keep his forces under U.S. command in an independent army. Germany's victories, however, forced the commander to bend his rules. In late April Pershing sent the U.S. First Division, numbering 28,000 men, to help the French army halt the German advance.

The doughboys joined French troops in two miles of trenches facing Cantigny, a German-occupied village northeast of Paris. On May 28 they were ordered to make their first offensive of the war. At dawn the soldiers climbed out of their trenches and marched across the broken ground, braving enemy shells and machine-gun fire. They captured Cantigny, along with two hundred German prisoners.

The assault was only a skirmish compared to the war's many brutal battles, but it proved the Americans' fighting spirit. "Bravo, the young Americans!" a London newspaper cheered. To General Pershing, "it was a matter of pride . . . that the troops of this division, in their first battle, . . . displayed the fortitude and courage of veterans."

Devil Dogs of Belleau Wood

While the doughboys stormed Cantigny, the Germans were continuing their drive toward Paris. American troops joined the Allies rushed to the front to stop them.

On May 31 the U.S. Third Division reached Château-Thierry on the Marne River. The town's French defenders were under heavy attack. The Americans reinforced the shattered French lines and halted the German advance.

Meanwhile, the U.S. Second Division, made up of infantrymen and marines, dug a shallow line of trenches in nearby Belleau Wood. The Germans struck on

The Spanish Flu

While troops fought and died in the final months of the war in Europe, another killer was stalking the American homefront: the Spanish flu. This deadly strain of influenza virus had made its first appearance in March 1918 at an army camp in Kansas. Within days, hundreds of soldiers were bedridden with sore throats, aches, and fever, often leading to pneumonia. Altogether, the flu would strike one of every four men in U.S. army camps and kill more than 600,000 Americans, both at home and abroad.

American soldiers carried the Spanish flu to Europe, and from there it spread around the globe. Germany was hit especially hard. Weakened by food shortages, more than 580,000 German soldiers and civilians caught the flu and perished. By the time the epidemic ran its course in early 1919, an estimated 20 million people worldwide had died from the Spanish flu. That was more than twice the number killed in combat in World War I.

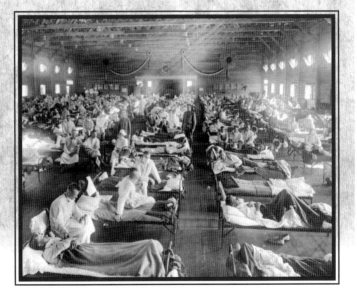

Flu victims crowd an emergency hospital at a Kansas army camp in 1918.

June 2. Marine rifle fire stopped them cold. Four days later, the Americans began a counterattack.

"Five minutes before five o'clock, the order for the advance reached our pit," recalled newspaperman Floyd Gibbons, traveling with the troops.

> There are really no heroics about it. There is no bugle call, no sword waving, no theatricalism—it's just plain get up and go over. . . . But with the appearance of our first line, as it stepped from the shelter of the woods into the open exposure of the flat field, the woods opposite began to crackle and rattle with the enemy machine gun fire.

The Germans had turned the square mile of woodland into a fortress, with three lines of trenches and "a machine gun to every wood-pile." Over the next three weeks, wave after wave of attackers charged into the slaughter. The ground was crowded with the dead. Americans and Germans lay side by side, their bodies torn apart by shells, bullets, and bayonets.

Finally, on June 25, the last German defenders retreated. More than five thousand Americans had been killed or wounded, nearly two-thirds of them marines. Impressed by the "kill or be killed" determination of the attackers, the Germans nicknamed the marines of Belleau Wood "Devil Dogs."

AFTER THE BATTLE OF BELLEAU WOOD, INFANTRYMAN LAMBERT WOOD OF THE U.S. NINTH INFANTRY REGIMENT, SECOND DIVISION, WROTE TO HIS PARENTS ABOUT THE PART HIS COMPANY OF MACHINE GUNNERS HAD PLAYED IN STOPPING THE GERMAN PUSH TOWARD PARIS. WOOD WAS KILLED IN ACTION FOUR DAYS LATER NEAR SOISSONS, FRANCE.

July 14, 1918

Dearest Folks:
Still out thank Heaven, hope we get a good long rest, we need it. We have had many wonderful things said about us, by the Great General [Pershing], by the Conventions of Mayors of the French towns we saved and by statesmen. . . . The hardships and dangers we endured and they were not light, seem as nothing to the thought that we were among

those few thousand devoted Americans who saved Paris and perhaps the whole outcome of the war. We do not talk much about it, but deep in our hearts we believe it. . . .

I started this letter hours ago, but have had so many brother officers dropping in for visits that I could not finish. We are so happy to see each other again and so childishly glad to be alive. It is such a fine feeling to know that you are respected and liked by these officers, who belong to the best fighting regiment of the best division in the American Expeditionary Forces, and all of whom have been tested in the fire of real battles and have not been found wanting, and to know that you, yourself, have done your part. We are almost like children laughing and talking and kidding one another. . . .

Do you know, dad, here I am commanding the Machine Gun Company in probably the most famous regiment in the army? One that has fought here almost continuously since early in March and not so long ago responsibility frightened me; but this comes almost as a matter of course; one's shoulders broaden when a load has been put on them and experience is surely the greatest teacher of all. Father, what college in the world could fit a man to shoulder the weight of leading so many men to battle, and in battle, in so important a branch as the M.G. [machine gunners] at an age of a little over twenty-three? . . .

Love to all and write often, please. Don't worry, I am so busy I don't get time to get killed.

Love,
Lambert

Attack and Counterattack

In July 1918 German commanders prepared for a *Friedensturm*, or "final peace offensive." In the four months since the start of their spring offensives, they had lost nearly 600,000 men. Fresh American forces were arriving at the rate of nearly a quarter million each month. Before the Germans were completely outnumbered, they hoped to win the war with one final, massive attack.

German soldiers who were captured by the Allies revealed the exact hour of the planned assault: midnight on July 15. When the storm troopers charged from their trenches, a huge force of French, British, Italian, and American troops was waiting.

The German advance quickly stalled. By the morning of July 18, it had turned into a retreat.

"Folks, we have them on the run," doughboy Charles Hershey wrote home. "I hope we keep them to it." With the Germans on the defensive, the Allies launched a counterattack. By September, losses on each side numbered nearly half a million. The Germans had been pushed back fifteen miles behind the lines they had held in March.

All through this period American divisions had fought under French command. Still, General Pershing had not lost sight of his plan to organize a separate U.S. army. There were now more than a million American troops in France. On August 10 Pershing gave them a new name: the U.S. First Army. Later that month the army moved into position for its first all-American offensive.

"As we were now about to enter into an active campaign," Pershing wrote, "the thought came to me, perhaps as never before, that many an American boy would . . . be buried on the battlefield before the contest in which we were engaged should come to an end." Many of the doughboys under his command had equally somber thoughts. Infantry officer Martin Hogan overheard this conversation:

> "This time tomorrow where will we be?" shouted someone.
> "Back in rest camp," another answered.
> "Like fun," exclaimed a lieutenant. "You'll be sprouting daisies maybe."

Saint-Mihiel: "One Fine Fight"

The American objective was a bulge jutting sixteen miles into the Allied lines near the French town of Saint-Mihiel. The Germans had held this pocket of land since 1914. Pershing planned to nip it off and straighten out the line.

A total of 550,000 Americans and 110,000 French support troops gathered for the assault. On September 12 they hit the enemy with a 3,200-gun artillery bombardment that sounded to one doughboy like "all the thunderstorms that ever happened on this old globe." Then the soldiers scrambled over the top of their trenches. Nearly 1,500 Allied planes—the largest concentration of airpower yet—swooped low over the advancing infantrymen. The planes strafed the opposing troops and signaled enemy positions for the American artillery.

Just before the assault began, the Germans had begun to withdraw from the Saint-Mihiel region. Caught in the middle of their march, some fought back fiercely, while others quickly surrendered. Within forty-eight hours, nearly all resistance had crumbled. Pershing's army cleared out the Germans and captured about 16,000 prisoners and 450 artillery pieces.

TWO NEW TOOLS OF WARFARE PLAYED AN IMPORTANT ROLE IN THE BATTLE OF SAINT-MIHIEL: THE AIRPLANE AND THE TANK. WHILE COMBAT PLANES SUPPORTED AMERICAN TROOPS FROM THE AIR, HUNDREDS OF TANKS ROLLED BEFORE AND ALONGSIDE THEM, FLATTENING THE ENEMY'S DEFENSES AND BLASTING MACHINE-GUN NESTS. COMMANDING ONE BRIGADE OF LIGHT TANKS WAS THIRTY-TWO-YEAR-OLD COLONEL GEORGE S. PATTON, WHO WOULD LATER BECOME ONE OF THE MOST FAMOUS GENERALS OF WORLD WAR II.

September 20 1918

Dear Papa

We have all been in one fine fight and it was not half so exciting as I had hoped. . . . When the shelling first started I had some doubts . . . , but it is just like taking a cold bath, once you get in, it is all right. . . .

The infantry were held up at a town so I happened to find some tanks and sent them through it I walked behind and some boshe [Germans] surrendered to me. At the next town all but one tank was out of sight and as the infantry would not go in I got on top of the tank to hearten the driver and we went in, that was most exciting as there were plenty of boshe we took thirty.

On leaving the town I was still sitting sidewise on top of the tank with my legs hanging down on the left side when all at once I noticed all the paint start to chip off the other side and at the same time I noticed machine guns. I dismounted in haste and got in a shell hole, which was none too large every time I started to get out the boshe shot at me. I was on the point of getting scared as I was about a hundred yards [ahead] of the [infantry] and all alone in the field. If I went back the infantry would think I was running and there was no reason to go forward alone. All the time the infernal tank was going on alone as the men had not noticed my hurried departure. At last the bright thought occurred to me that I could move across the front in an oblique [indirect] direction and not appear to run yet at the same time get back. This I did listening for the machine guns with all my ears, and laying down in a great hurry when I heard them, in this manner I hoped to beat the bullets to me. Sometime I will figure the speed of sounds and bullets and see if I was right. It is the only use I know of that math has ever been to me.

I found the Major of the infantry and asked him if he would come on after the tank. He would not as the next battalion on his left had not come up (he was killed ten minutes later) Then I drew a long breath and went after the tank on foot as I could not let it be going against a whole town alone. It is strange but quite true that at this time I was not the least scared, as I had the idea of getting the tank fixed in my head. I did not even fear the bullets though I could see the guns spitting at me, I did however run like H—— On reaching the tank about four hundred yards out in the field I tapped on the back door with my stick, and thank God it was a long one. The sergeant looked out and saluted and said what do you want now Colonel, I told him to turn and come back he was much depressed. . . .

Then I walked along the battle front to see how the left battalion had gotten on. It was a very long way and I had had no sleep for four nights and no food all the day as I lost my sack chasing a boshe, I got some crackers off a dead one. . . . It was most interesting over the battle field like the books but much less dramatic. The dead were about mostly hit in the head. There were a lot of our men stripping off buttons and other things but they always covered the face of the dead in a nice way. . . .

much love to all

Your devoted son

Meuse-Argonne: The Final Push

After its success at Saint-Mihiel, the U.S. First Army raced to a new battlefront. The Allies were planning a major offensive, with strikes at different points all along the western front. American troops were assigned to a region stretching twenty miles from the Meuse River west to the Argonne Forest.

A recruiting poster for the U.S. Tank Corps. First developed by the British in 1915, tanks became an important tool of modern warfare.

The attack began on September 26, 1918. At first, the doughboys made rapid progress, charging across no-man's-land and capturing the enemy's first line of defenses. Then German reinforcements arrived. The American advance stalled in a wilderness of dense woods, steep hills, and narrow valleys, all fortified with an elaborate system of trenches and earthen barriers.

Sergeant William Langer described the scene after the first day of the battle.

> Trees, as well as the underbrush, had been shot away or left in a charred condition. The entire area was covered with fields of barbed wire and cut in all directions with great trench systems or dugouts. . . . The shellfire and mine explosions . . . left the whole landscape torn and scarred. . . . Imagine the ocean at its roughest and then imagine it instantly changed into clay.

U.S. troops began their advance in the Argonne Forest in thick fog. One doughboy described the scene as "the weirdest panorama of mist and mystery that mortal imagination could conjure up."

For days the doughboys struggled across this broken, lethal terrain. Thousands were cut down by enemy artillery and machine gunners hidden among the rocks and thickets. The men were pelted with rain and sleet. Food, ammunition, and other supplies fell behind them as they ground their way slowly forward.

At the beginning of October, fresh troops arrived. The Americans continued to force the Germans back, step by bloody step. "The men were holding on determinedly," recalled infantry officer Joseph Lawrence, "but were in bad shape—hungry, wet, caked from head to foot with mud and filth, suffering from dysentery [diarrhea]."

The Lost Battalion

One of the most famous stories of World War I involved an infantry unit known as the "Lost Battalion." On October 2, 1918, 679 men from two U.S. battalions pushed ahead of other American forces advancing in the Argonne Forest. By nightfall, they were cut off, two miles deep in enemy territory and surrounded by the Germans.

Huddled in shallow shell holes, the doughboys held off the enemy for six days. "It rained almost constantly," recalled Lieutenant Maurice Griffin,

> *and we wallowed in mud. . . . We had no rations and were forced to eat brush, leaves and roots. . . . The Germans crept up on us and made five attacks while we were cut off, but we silenced each attack. . . . They would occasionally throw over a hand grenade. Sometimes we could toss them back before they exploded.*

By October 7, the remaining soldiers from the combined battalions were weak with hunger and exhaustion, their ammunition nearly gone. Finally, American troops broke through to them. There were 252 survivors. Asked how he felt after being rescued, the Lost Battalion's leader, Major Charles Whittlesey, responded, "Rescue, hell. . . . If you had come up when we did, you wouldn't have put us in that fix."

By the middle of the month, 75,000 doughboys had been lost in the Meuse-Argonne. The fighting had reached the Hindenburg Line—Germany's last line of defense. A fresh assault on November 1 forced the enemy back across the Meuse River. "We started after them again the next morning," recalled one infantryman, "and found—they had 'flown the coop.' "

The exhausted soldiers could not know it, but peace was just days away.

Collapse of the Central Powers

As fighting raged in the Meuse-Argonne, British, French, and Belgian troops were pounding German forces farther north on the western front. Germany's partner nations were also failing fast. The Allied blockade had reduced the Central Powers to near-starvation. Between the end of September and the beginning of November, Bulgaria, Turkey, and Austria-Hungary all surrendered.

Germany and the Allies sign the armistice ending World War I, November 11, 1918.

Now Germany stood alone. Its people were demanding an end to war, and its government was tottering. The German navy mutinied and the army was in retreat. On November 9 the nation's leader, Kaiser Wilhelm II, abdicated (gave up the throne), and a new government took power. German delegates met with France's General Ferdinand Foch to discuss the terms of an armistice, or truce.

ON THE NIGHT BEFORE THE SIGNING OF THE ARMISTICE ENDING WORLD WAR I, SUPPLY OFFICER SYLVESTER BUTLER WROTE DOWN HIS THOUGHTS ON THE ROLE THE UNITED STATES HAD PLAYED IN THE ALLIED VICTORY.

Nov. 10, 1918

Dear Mother,

Today, the papers say the Kaiser is to abdicate; the German chancellor talks in the past tense about Germany's being no longer able to keep up the struggle against ever-increasing forces; to-morrow the German delegates at the armistice conference must accept or reject Foch's terms. . . . What marvellous things have happened in the last three months! The French feel seemingly a sort of wondering joy over the turn things have taken, and all say generously "It's because you Americans have come", without us the war would have lasted ten years, probably lost. It is very satisfying and heart-warming to hear them say it. . . . It was America's throwing of her might into the scale against Prussian brutality & selfish ambitions, which saved the world from it. I am . . . absolutely convinced of it. Our part physically does not seem so large, though surely what has been done in such a short time is marvelous, and our troops hold the most difficult section of the front; but the moral force of our entry alone has counted tremendously, first, that we showed our colors, we gave the judgment of the greatest disinterested [impartial] nation of the world that the Allies were fighting a battle for the world & civilization against brute force & evil; second, the mere fact that we were coming gave our war weary allies new courage to hold on during 1917, the waiting year, and the terrible anxious days of last spring; and this fall, our troops I am convinced, made possible the great general allied advance which has ended so gloriously, though at a tremendous cost. . . .

Lots of love to all.

Sylvester

The Eleventh Hour

"All of a sudden our artillery stopped firing," recalled infantryman Connell Albertine.

> We were all up on our feet wondering just what had happened. . . .
> Looking directly to our rear where our artillery was, we saw some
> French artillerymen throwing their helmets in the air. Then at this
> moment—and what a moment—one that will live with us as long
> as we live—an officer from G Company came running down the
> trench, practically breathless and very excited, shouting, "The war
> is over . . . the war is over . . . an armistice has been signed."

Allied soldiers celebrate victory and the coming of peace.

Peace came at the "eleventh hour": 11:00 A.M., November 11, 1918. At first, many Americans at the front simply could not believe it. "We had hoped so long and passionately for this hour to come," remembered ambulance driver Guy Bowerman, "that our minds could not grasp the meaning of it when it was here."

As the news sank in, soldiers and civilians on both sides reacted with relief and joy. Lieutenant Walter Davenport watched as German troops climbed from their trenches in the Meuse-Argonne and "began to shout wildly. They threw their rifles, hats, . . . bayonets and trench knives toward us. They began to sing." Flares, rockets, and bonfires lit the skies. "The whole front," wrote Lieutenant Frederick Sullivan, "was blazing like a grand Fourth of July celebration."

Elsewhere, the celebrations were quieter. "You can't imagine the feelings of the boys," doughboy Ira Schubert wrote to a friend back in Chicago. "The only way they could celebrate the victory was to pat each other on the back and thank Almighty God that they survived the greatest ordeal man ever went through."

It would be long months before the last of the American Expeditionary Force returned home. While they waited their turn, the doughboys helped rebuild Europe's shattered war zones. They marched and drilled, and they griped about army regulations, their worn-out shoes, and their growing restlessness and boredom. Many also searched for meaning in the war's terrible costs and sacrifices.

"Now that it is all over, what is there to look back upon?" asked pilot Lewis Plush aboard a troopship bound for America.

> Men fought to kill, to maim, to destroy. Some return home, others remain behind forever on the fields of their greatest sacrifice. The rewards of the dead are the lasting honors of martyrs for humanity; the reward of the living is the peaceful conscience of one who plays the game of life and plays it square.

Conclusion

A Costly Peace

World War I had lasted four and a half years. Estimates of its costs vary widely, but by any measurement, they were staggering. Roughly 8 million soldiers had lost their lives. Another 20 million had been wounded, many suffering permanent disabilities. The war was also responsible for the deaths of somewhere from 6 million to 10 million civilians.

Most of these losses took place in Europe. The world war also brought battles, death, and destruction to European colonies in the Pacific Ocean, the Middle East, Asia, and Africa. Several countries that never saw combat suffered the loss of soldiers sent in support of the Allies. These included Australia, Canada, New Zealand, and, of course, the United States. American deaths numbered about 116,000. Of these, 53,000 died from combat, 63,000 from disease and other causes.

Along with its human toll, World War I had far-reaching economic and political consequences. The warring nations had lost hundreds of billions of dollars. Most would suffer long periods of poverty, hunger, and economic upheaval. At the same time, old political systems had collapsed. The Austro-Hungarian Empire had ceased to exist, and communism had taken root in Russia. The series of peace treaties negotiated after the war changed the map of Europe, creating

An American soldier stands amid the ruins in war-shattered France.

new nations and dealing out territories from the conquered Central Powers to the victorious Allies. In the process, the peace settlements planted the seeds for further conflict.

Months before the war's end, President Woodrow Wilson had outlined a plan for peace called the Fourteen Points. Wilson's proposals included openness and fair dealing among nations, respect for the rights of all peoples to self-government, and establishment of an organization of nations to settle future disputes peacefully. After the armistice Wilson traveled to Europe. He wanted to make certain his ideals were represented in the peace conference held in the suburbs outside Paris. But the president found that the other Allied nations were determined to punish Germany with a harsh settlement.

The Treaty of Versailles was signed on June 28, 1919. Its terms were a bitter humiliation for the German people. Germany was forced to accept the blame for starting the war. It had to give up some of its territories to other nations and drastically reduce its armed forces. Most damaging of all, it was required to repay the Allies for their war losses, in an amount eventually set at $33 billion.

The treaty also established President Wilson's proposed League of Nations. In a strange twist, though, the United States never became a member.

America had been one of the few nations to emerge from World War I stronger than before. Thanks to wartime production and trade, its economy was booming. The U.S. Army and Navy had grown into first-rate forces. In fact, in the postwar years the United States would become the most powerful nation in the world. However, President Wilson's political rivals, who controlled the U.S. Congress, were isolationists. They feared that membership in the League of Nations would once again draw the country into foreign conflicts. By refusing to ratify the Treaty of Versailles, they made it impossible for the United States to join the league. Over the next two decades, U.S. political leaders would do their best to steer clear of European affairs.

Europe had been left weakened and divided by the war and its aftermath. The people of nations on both sides of the conflict felt angry and betrayed by their losses in territory and the failure of their allies to keep wartime promises. Nowhere was there more bitterness than in Germany. Within twenty years, the burdens imposed by the Treaty of Versailles would topple that nation's government. The German people's rage and shame would lead to the rise of the Nazi party. The conclusion of the "war to end all wars" had created conditions that would lead to the even greater devastations of World War II. That conflict would draw the United States out of isolation once and for all, to take a leading role on the world's stage.

Time Line of World War I Events

1914

JUNE 28
Archduke Franz Ferdinand is assassinated in Bosnia by a Serbian nationalist.

JULY 28
Austria-Hungary declares war on Serbia.

AUGUST 1–3
Germany declares war on Russia and France.

AUGUST 4–5
Great Britain declares war on Germany. Germany invades Belgium. Austria-Hungary declares war on Russia.

AUGUST 10–12
Great Britain and France declare war on Austria-Hungary.

SEPTEMBER 5–10
The First Battle of the Marne: French forces turn back Germany's attempt to overrun France.

SEPTEMBER 15
First trenches are dug along the western front.

OCTOBER 20– NOVEMBER 24
First Battle of Ypres: British troops stop German advance through Flanders toward the North Sea.

OCTOBER 31
Turkish Empire joins the Central Powers.

NOVEMBER 2–5
Russia, Great Britain, and France declare war on Turkey.

1915

FEBRUARY 4
Germany proclaims the waters surrounding Great Britain a war zone.

APRIL 22
Germans launch the first poison gas attack, against French-Algerian troops in Belgium.

MAY 7
A German submarine torpedoes and sinks the British passenger liner *Lusitania*.

MAY 23
Italy enters the war on the side of the Allies.

1916

FEBRUARY 21
Germany attacks the French city of Verdun.

MAY 31
Battle of Jutland between the British and German fleets in the North Sea.

JULY 1
The British and French begin a large-scale attack along the Somme River in northwest France.

AUGUST 28
Italy declares war on Germany.

OCTOBER 29
Turkey declares war on the Allies.

NOVEMBER 7
President Woodrow Wilson is elected to a second term.

NOVEMBER 18
Battle of the Somme ends with 650,000 German, 420,000 British, and 195,000 French casualties.

1917

JANUARY 8
The Allies withdraw in defeat from Turkey's Gallipoli Peninsula.

FEBRUARY 1
Germany resumes unrestricted submarine warfare in British waters.

MARCH 15
Czar Nicholas II abdicates after revolution breaks out in Russia.

APRIL 6
The United States declares war on Germany.

MAY 18
The Selective Service Act becomes law in the United States.

OCTOBER 24– NOVEMBER 12
The Central Powers rout the Italians at the Battle of Caporetto.

NOVEMBER 10
Britain ends the Third Battle of Ypres, after losses estimated at between 250,000 and 400,000.

DECEMBER 15
Russia signs a truce with the Central Powers.

1918

JANUARY 8
President Wilson outlines his Fourteen Point plan for peace.

MARCH 11
Influenza breaks out at an army camp in Kansas.

MARCH 19
The U.S. Navy authorizes the first enlistment of women.

MARCH 21
Germany launches the first of five major offensives on the western front.

MAY 28
U.S. forces capture Cantigny, France.

JUNE 4
The battle between U.S. and German troops at Château-Thierry, France, ends in a U.S. victory.

JUNE 25
Battle of Belleau Wood ends in another U.S. victory.

JULY 15
Germany's final offensive begins.

JULY 18
The Allies halt the German offensive and begin a counterattack.

SEPTEMBER 12–16
The U.S. First Army defeats the Germans at Saint-Mihiel.

SEPTEMBER 26
The Meuse-Argonne offensive begins.

OCTOBER 30
Turkish Empire surrenders to the Allies.

NOVEMBER 3
Austria-Hungary surrenders to the Allies.

NOVEMBER 9
Kaiser Wilhelm II of Germany abdicates and flees into exile.

NOVEMBER 11
The armistice is signed and fighting ends on the western front.

1919

JUNE 28
Treaty of Versailles is signed in Paris.

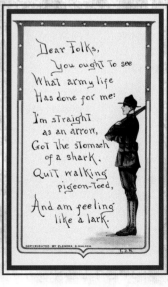

Dear Folks,
You ought to see
What army life
Has done for me:

I'm straight
as an arrow,
Got the stomach
of a shark.
Quit walking
pigeon-toed,

And am feeling
like a lark.

COPYRIGHTED BY ELENORA S.WALKER.

Glossary

battle cruiser A large warship that is lighter and faster than a battleship.

battleship A very large, well-armed warship.

blockade The act of blocking enemy ports to prevent imports and exports.

cavalry An army mounted on horseback.

Communist Following a political system in which all property is owned and controlled by the government.

conscription A military draft.

countersign A secret word or signal given by someone in order to pass a military guard.

destroyer A small, fast, heavily armed warship.

doughboy A slang term for an American soldier, which goes back to the Civil War but did not come into common use until World War I. The term comes from the small, round buttons on Union uniforms, which looked like flour dumplings or biscuits.

fuselage The central body of an airplane.

Hun A negative term for a German soldier; taken from the nomadic peoples of central Asia who conquered much of Europe in the fifth century.

infantry The foot soldiers of an army.

isolationist policy A policy in which a nation avoids international alliances and commitments.

no-man's-land The unoccupied area between the opposing trenches on the western front.

parapet A wall or mound of earth to protect soldiers.

propaganda Ideas or information, often untrue or misleading, spread by a government or an organization to influence public opinion.

storm troopers German infantry soldiers specially trained and equipped to penetrate quickly and deeply into enemy territory.

subchaser A small, fast patrol boat armed for attacking submarines.

tracers Machine-gun bullets that contain a chemical to make them glow during flight, as an aid in aiming.

U-boats German submarines.

To Find Out More

BOOKS

Cooper, Michael L. *Hell Fighters: African American Soldiers in World War I.* New York: Lodestar Books, 1997.
A lively account of the experiences of African-American combat soldiers in Europe.

George, Linda S. *World War I.* New York: Benchmark Books, 2002.
Companion title in the Letters from the Homefront series.

Heyman, Neil M. *World War I.* Guides to Historic Events of the Twentieth Century series. Westport, CT: Greenwood Press, 1997.
A comprehensive history written for high-school and college students; includes major events of the war, biographies of political and military figures, and selections from personal narratives, newspaper editorials, and government papers.

Pendergast, Tom, and Sara Pendergast. *World War I Almanac.* New York: Gale Group, 2002.
Covers the major events of the war, with chapters on special aspects such as combat at sea, technology, and the impact on civilians; also includes many black-and-white photos and maps, a glossary, a time line, and ideas for school reports and projects.

Ross, Stewart. *Causes and Consequences of World War I.* Austin, TX: Raintree Steck-Vaughn, 1998.
A concise account of events leading up to the war and U.S. involvement, plus the human, political, and economic costs; illustrated with a number of photographs and maps.

Sommerville, Donald. *World War I.* History of Warfare series. Austin, TX: Raintree Steck-Vaughn, 1999.
An easy-to-read look at the major events of the war, with chapters on air and sea combat and on battlefronts outside Europe.

Westwell, Ian. *World War I: Day by Day.* Osceola, WI: MBI Publishing, 2000.
A very detailed chronological history of the war, with some four hundred photos and maps.

ON THE INTERNET*

"American Heritage Center: For Home and Country in World War I (1914–1918)," © 2000 University of Wyoming, at http://uwadmnweb.uwyo.edu/AHC/exhibits/veterans/ww1.htm
The University of Wyoming's easy-to-navigate site covers the historical background of U.S. involvement in World War I, with articles on activities of the air service, army, and navy.

"The Doughboy Center," presented by The Great War Society and the Library of Congress Veterans History Project, © 1998 The Great War Society, at http://www.worldwar1.com/dbc
This is an excellent source of information on the American Expeditionary Force. Topics include major battles, naval and air operations, weapons and equipment, monuments and memorials, books and films, and much more. There are also numerous photographs and primary sources, including letters, diaries, and firsthand accounts.

*Websites change from time to time. For additional on-line information, check with the media specialist at your local library.

"First World War.com: The War to End All Wars," © 2000–2002 Michael Duffy, at http://www.firstworldwar.com

Articles offer information on the war's background, battles, and political and military leaders; the site also includes a time line, photographs, posters, and links to primary sources including diaries and firsthand accounts.

"Trenches on the Web: An Internet History of the Great War" at http://www.worldwar1.com/index.html

Designed for students, this website offers a wide variety of information on the people, places, and events of World War I. Click on "Reference Library" for a site map to help you find your way around the many articles and links.

"U.S.A.F. Museum: World War I History" at http://www.wpafb.af.mil/museum/history/ww1/ww1.htm

Based on exhibits at the U.S. Air Force Museum in Ohio, this is an excellent overview of the U.S. Army Air Service in World War I. The site includes a nine-minute video on the early days of combat aviation.

VIDEO

World War I: The Complete Story. Produced by CBS News, distributed by FoxVideo, 1994.

An excellent series, available on three videos; grainy, sometimes faded, always compelling film footage brings alive the stories of political intrigue and combat on land and sea and in the air.

Bibliography

Barbeau, Arthur E., and Florette Henri. *The Unknown Soldiers: Black American Troops in World War I.* Philadelphia: Temple University Press, 1974.

Berry, Henry. *Make the Kaiser Dance: Living Memories of the Doughboys.* New York: Arbor House, 1978.

Bosco, Peter I. *World War I.* New York: Facts on File, 1991.

Bowerman, Guy Emerson, Jr. *The Compensations of War: The Diary of an Ambulance Driver during the Great War.* Austin, TX: University of Texas Press, 1983.

Carroll, Andrew, ed. *War Letters: Extraordinary Correspondence from American Wars.* New York: Scribner, 2001.

Cooper, Michael L. *Hell Fighters: African American Soldiers in World War I.* New York: Lodestar Books, 1997.

Dolan, Edward F. *America in World War I.* Brookfield, CT: Millbrook Press, 1996.

Empey, Arthur Guy. *"Over the Top" by an American Soldier Who Went.* New York: G. P. Putnam's, 1917.

Ferrell, Robert H. *Woodrow Wilson & World War I, 1917–1921.* New York: Harper & Row, 1985.

Freidel, Frank. *Over There: The Story of America's First Great Overseas Crusade.* Boston: Little, Brown, 1964.

Hallas, James H., ed. *Doughboy War: The American Expeditionary Force in World War I.* Boulder, CO: Lynne Rienner Publishers, 2000.

Haythornthwaite, Philip J. *The World War One Source Book.* London: Brockhampton Press, 1992.

Henri, Florette. *Bitter Victory: A History of Black Soldiers in World War I.* Garden City, NY: Doubleday, 1970.

Heyman, Neil M. *World War I.* Westport, CT: Greenwood Press, 1997.

Langer, William L. *Gas and Flame in World War I.* New York: Alfred A. Knopf, 1965.

Lee, Arthur Gould. *No Parachute: A Fighter Pilot in World War I.* New York: Harper & Row, 1968.

Lewis, Jon E., ed. *The Mammoth Book of War Diaries & Letters: Life on the Battlefield in the Words of the Ordinary Soldier.* New York: Carroll & Graf, 1999.

Lyons, Michael J. *World War I: A Short History.* Englewood Cliffs, NJ: Prentice Hall, 1994.

Marshall, S. L. A., and the editors of American Heritage. *The American Heritage History of World War I.* New York: American Heritage Publishing Co., 1964.

Pendergast, Tom, and Sara Pendergast. *World War I Almanac.* New York: Gale Group, 2002.

Pershing, John J. *My Experiences in the First World War.* Vols. 1 and 2. New York: Da Capo Press, 1995.

Ross, Stewart. *Causes and Consequences of World War I.* Austin, TX: Raintree Steck-Vaughn, 1998.

Rote, Nelle Fairchild. "Nurse Helen Fairchild: My Aunt, My Hero." *Daughters of the American Revolution Magazine,* November 1997, vol. 131, no. 9. Reprinted at http://raven.cc.ukans.edu/~kansite/ww_one/medical/MaMh/MyAunt.htm

Sommerville, Donald. *World War I.* Austin, TX: Raintree Steck-Vaughn, 1999.

Stokesbury, James L. *A Short History of World War I.* New York: William Morrow, 1981.

Strachan, Hew, ed. *The Oxford Illustrated History of the First World War.* New York: Oxford University Press, 1998.

Taussig, Joseph Knefler. *The Queenstown Patrol, 1917: The Diary of Commander Joseph Knefler Taussig, U.S. Navy.* Edited by William N. Still, Jr. Newport, RI: Naval War College Press, 1996.

Thoumin, Richard. *The First World War.* New York: G. P. Putnam's, 1964.

Villard, Henry S., and James Nagel. *Hemingway in Love and War: The Lost Diary of Agnes von Kurowsky, Her Letters, and Correspondence of Ernest Hemingway.* Boston: Northeastern University Press, 1989.

Westwell, Ian. *World War I: Day by Day.* Osceola, WI: MBI Publishing, 2000.

Notes on Quotes

The quotes in this book are from the following sources:

Chapter One: The Reluctant Warrior

p. 8, "In the history": Heyman, *World War I,* p. 187.

p. 8, "[We] need only" and "a struggle": ibid., p. 186.

p. 10, "plucky little Belgium": Haythornthwaite, *World War One Source Book,* p. 148.

p. 12, "violation of many": Marshall, *American Heritage,* p. 145.

p. 15, "I can't keep": "The Millennial Files Archives: 20th Century," at
http://www.mmmfiles.com/archive/ww1uspart.htm

p. 17, "There is no question": Marshall, *American Heritage,* p. 204.

p. 17, "The world must be made": "President Woodrow Wilson's War Message" at
http://www.lib.byu.edu/~rdh/wwi/1917/wilswarm.html

Chapter Two: Yanks at War

p. 18, "Over there": Bosco, *World War I,* p. 63.

p. 18, "On the 14th": Hallas, *Doughboy War,* p. 8.

p. 20, "fired by patriotic": Villard and Nagel, *Hemingway in Love and War,* p. 1.

p. 20, "We could picture": Hallas, *Doughboy War,* p. 9.

p. 20, "in no sense": Freidel, *Over There,* p. 10.

p. 20, "All of us": Hallas, *Doughboy War,* p. 24.

p. 20, "long, hollow, wooden": ibid., p. 26.

p. 21, "We get up": Freidel, *Over There,* pp. 15, 17.

p. 22, "We're ready": ibid., p. 45.

p. 22, "spellbound by the wonder": Hallas, *Doughboy War,* p. 34.

p. 23, "a long jump": Bowerman, *Compensations of War*, p. 9.

p. 23, "bridge of ships": Freidel, *Over There*, p. 65.

p. 23, "We marched": Hallas, *Doughboy War*, p. 42.

p. 24, "looked like a moving": Pershing, *My Experiences*, vol. 1, p. 92.

p. 24, *"Lafayette, nous voici!"* Haythornthwaite, *World War One Source Book*, p. 309.

p. 24, "a successful offensive": Pershing, *My Experiences*, vol. 1, p. 80.

p. 27, "haphazard melange" and "There was hardly": Hallas, *Doughboy War*, p. 65.

p. 30, "A horse": ibid., p. 180.

p. 32, "decided to go": Lewis, *Mammoth Book*, pp. 347, 348.

pp. 32–33, "I was talking": Freidel, *Over There*, p. 128.

Chapter Three: At Sea and in the Air

p. 34, "The duration": Freidel, *Over There*, p. 219.

p. 36, "cooperate fully": Taussig, *Queenstown Patrol*, p. 16.

p. 37, "submarine smashing game": ibid., p. 38.

p. 37, "The most tense": Freidel, *Over There*, pp. 37–38.

p. 37, "small but mighty" and "many thrilling": ibid., pp. 43, 44.

p. 38, "It was the policy": ibid., p. 40.

p. 38, "good eye": ibid., p. 152.

p. 39, "Here one could": ibid., p. 156.

p. 40, "I heard a sort": ibid., pp. 159–160.

p. 40, "The day of days": Lee, *No Parachute*, pp. 10, 13.

p. 42, "I have seen": Freidel, *Over There*, p. 147.

p. 42, "airborne warriors": Lee, *No Parachute*, p. xv.

p. 43, "ordinary young men": ibid., p. xviii.

p. 43, "neither chance nor mood": ibid., p. xvi.

Chapter Four: African Americans and Women at War

p. 46, "If the colored": Henri, *Bitter Victory*, p. 88.

p. 47, "Millions of negroes": Barbeau, *Unknown Soldiers*, pp. 34–35.

p. 48, "Colored troops": ibid., pp. 90, 91.

p. 48, "five thousand tons": ibid., pp. 103–104.

p. 50, "rank cowards": ibid., p. 154.

p. 51, "mixed up": Hallas, *Doughboy War*, pp. 20–21.

p. 51, "I sought": ibid., p. 22.

p. 52, "superb spirit": Barbeau, *Unknown Soldiers*, p. 131.

p. 52, "We return": "We Shall Overcome: W. E. B. Du Bois Boyhood Homesite," at http://www.cr.nps.gov/nr/travel/civilrights/ma2.htm

p. 55, "The cannon": Freidel, *Over There*, p. 267.

p. 56, "a sort of coal-cellar": ibid.

p. 56, "We all live": Rote, "Nurse Helen Fairchild."

p. 56, "somehow the girls": Freidel, *Over There,* p. 313.

p. 56, "both wonderful organizations": Lewis, *Mammoth Book,* p. 339.

Chapter Five: The Tide Turns toward Victory

p. 58, "Last night": Freidel, *Over There,* p. 198.

p. 60, "Bravo, the young": Marshall, *American Heritage,* p. 305.

p. 60, "it was a matter": Pershing, *My Experiences,* vol. 2, p. 60.

p. 62, "Five minutes": Hallas, *Doughboy War,* p. 88.

p. 62, "a machine gun": ibid., p. 90.

p. 64, "Folks, we have": Freidel, *Over There,* p. 199.

p. 64, "As we were": Pershing, *My Experiences,* vol. 2, p. 257.

p. 64, "This time": Hallas, *Doughboy War,* p. 227.

p. 64, "all the thunderstorms": ibid.

p. 68, "Trees, as well": Langer, *Gas and Flame,* p. 52.

p. 69, "The men were holding": Hallas, *Doughboy War,* p. 282.

p. 69, "It rained": ibid., p. 260.

p. 69, "Rescue, hell": ibid., p. 263.

p. 70, "We started": Freidel, *Over There,* p. 327.

p. 72, "All of a sudden": Hallas, *Doughboy War,* p. 305.

p. 73, "We had hoped": Bowerman, *Compensations of War,* p. 164.

p. 73, "began to shout": Freidel, *Over There,* p. 350.

p. 73, "The whole front": ibid., p. 351.

p. 73, "You can't imagine": Carroll, *War Letters,* p. 167.

p. 73, "Now that it": ibid., pp. 168, 170.

Acknowledgments

Every effort has been made to trace the copyright holders of the letters reprinted in this book. We apologize for any omissions or errors in this regard and would be pleased to make the appropriate acknowledgments in any future printings.

Grateful acknowledgments are made to the following historical societies, libraries, publishers, and individuals:

Ernest Cowper to Elbert Hubbard II, March 12, 1916. From Hubbard, Elbert II. *The Selected Writings of Elbert Hubbard: The Roycrofters, 1928.* New York: Wm. H. Wise & Co., 1928.

"Zimmermann telegram," January 19, 1917. From the National Archives and Records Administration, State Department Central Decimal File 862.20212 (German espionage in Mexico), 1910–1929.

Lester Hensler to his parents. From Carroll, Andrew, ed. *War Letters: Extraordinary Correspondence from American Wars.* New York: Scribner, 2001.

Floyd Gibbons narrative. From Gibbons, Floyd. *"And They Thought We Wouldn't Fight!"* New York: George H. Doran, 1918.

Paul Hendrickson to his parents, September 10, 1918. Reprinted by permission of Jim and Betty (Hendrickson) Gill.

Roy Bainbridge to his mother, July 18, 1918. Courtesy of the Kansas State Historical Society.

Joseph Taussig diary, May 6, 1917. Joseph K. Taussig Papers, Manuscript Register Series No. 18, Naval Historical Collection Division, Naval War College, Newport, Rhode Island.

Jack Morris Wright to his mother, September 11, 1917. From *A Poet of the Air: Letters of Jack Morris Wright, First Lieutenant of the American Aviation in France, April 1917–January 1918.* Edited by Sara Greene Wise. Boston: Houghton & Mifflin, 1918.

Arthur Gould Lee to his wife, June 2, 1917. From Lee, Arthur Gould. *No Parachute: A Fighter Pilot in World War I.* New York: Harper & Row, 1968.

Committee of 100 Citizens on the War to Woodrow Wilson, May 11, 1917. Woodrow Wilson Papers, Series 4, file 152, Library of Congress, Washington, D.C.

"Mademoiselle Miss" letter, October 8, 1915. From *"Mademoiselle Miss": Letters from an American Girl Serving with the Rank of Lieutenant in a French Army Hospital at the Front.* Boston: W. A. Butterfield, 1916.

Lambert Wood to his parents, July 14, 1918. From Wilmot, Mrs. Frank. *Oregon Boys in the War.* Portland, OR: Glass & Prudhomme Co., 1918.

George S. Patton to his father, September 20, 1918. George S. Patton Papers, Manuscript Division, Library of Congress, Washington, D.C.

Sylvester Butler to his mother, November 10, 1918. From "The Doughboy Center," presented by The Great War Society and the Library of Congress Veterans History Project, © 1998 The Great War Society, at http://www.worldwar1.com/dbc

Index

Page numbers for illustrations are in boldface

About the Author

"After researching and writing books for the *Letters from the Homefront* series, it was fascinating to take a look at America's wars from a different point of view in *Letters from the Battlefront.* While I read the let-  ters, diaries, and reflections of soldiers from the American Revolution all the way through the Vietnam War, I was struck once again by the way, in our fast-changing world, people themselves remain so little changed. The Continental soldier shivering at Valley Forge and the army infantry-man in the jungles of South Vietnam wore differ-ent uniforms and carried different weapons. They sometimes used different words to express their feelings. But beneath the skin, their basic concerns and emotions—their love of life, their longing for home and family, their search for meaning amid the bewildering inhumanity of war—were startlingly similar."

VIRGINIA SCHOMP has written more than forty books on nonfiction topics including ancient cultures and American history. Ms. Schomp lives in the Catskill Mountain region of New York with her husband, Richard, and their son, Chip.